The

of Being a
BRILLIANT
TEENAGER

The Art of

Being a

BRILLIANT

TEENAGER

Andy Cope
Amy Bradley

CAPSTONE
A Wiley Brand

Registered Office(s)
John Wiley & Sons Ltd, The Atrium, Southern Gate, Chichester, West Sussex, PO19 8SQ, UK
John Wiley & Sons, Inc., 111 River Street, Hoboken, NJ 07030, USA
John Wiley & Sons Singapore Pte. Ltd, 1 Fusionopolis Walk, #06-01 Solaris South Tower, Singapore 138628

Editorial Office
The Atrium, Southern Gate, Chichester, West Sussex, PO19 8SQ, UK

For details of our global editorial offices, customer services, and more information about Wiley products visit us at www.wiley.com.

Wiley also publishes its books in a variety of electronic formats and by print-on-demand. Some content that appears in standard print versions of this book may not be available in other formats.

Library of Congress Cataloging-in-Publication Data is Available.

ISBN 9780857089397 (Paperback)
ISBN 9780857089410 (ePDF)
ISBN 9780857089403 (ePub)

Cover Design: Amy Bradley

Printed in Great Britain by Bell and Bain Ltd, Glasgow

DEDICATION (AND PLOT SPOILER)

Three little words of truth for all the young humans who read this book:

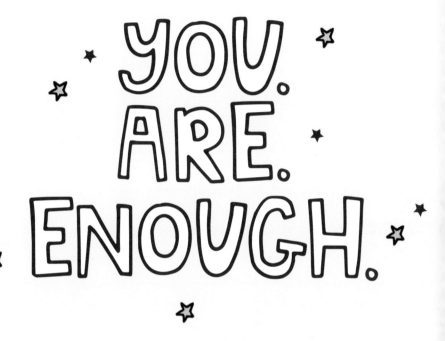

YOU. ARE. ENOUGH.

SPESH THANKS TO:

Darrell Woodman & Andy Whittaker.

Brilliant trainers and amazing people. Guys, thanks for helping out with the original version of the book.

CONTENTS

Real life doesn't come at you in chapters. It's full of lessons, ideas, challenges, questions, lightbulb moments, arguments, discussions and ultimatums.

Welcome to the book that prepares you for REAL life.

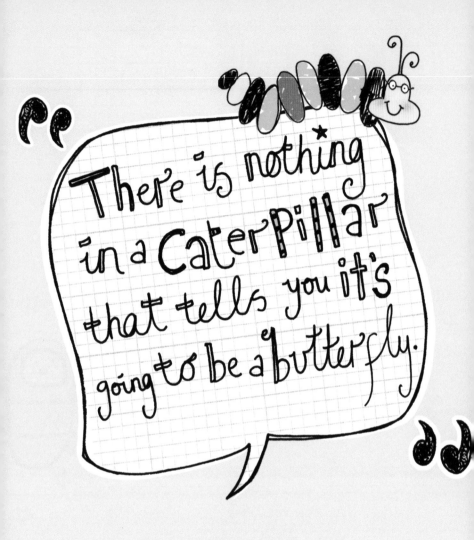

There is nothing in a CaterPillar that tells you it's going to be a butterfly.

Buckminster Fuller

American writer and futurist

Chapter 1.

Truths, half-truths and nothing like the truth

Pride, dazzle or grunt?

Famously, fish live in schools, sheep in flocks and cows in herds. There are armies of ants and lions hang around in a pride. But the best collective nouns are the lesser known ones; a tower of giraffes, a flamboyance of flamingos and, my all-time favourite, a *dazzle* of zebras.

For the record, the collective noun for teenagers is a 'grunt'. Apologies for the terrible stereotype but, hey, don't shoot the messenger! I didn't invent it, I'm just reporting it.

But it begs the question, what description would you choose for yourself and your tribe?

A bravery, a risk, a determination, maybe? Or a boredom, sulk or grumble? You could be a hope, disappointment, energy, creativity, joy, blessing, pain, pleasure, disruption... or all of the above.

One thing you definitely are is *potential* and, plot spoiler, this book is 100% about that.

But before you get started, I need a quick word about how the book works. The aim was to write a book that ticks all the teenage coming-of-age boxes, *and so much more!*

Life is like Mario Kart. There are a lot of crazy characters jostling for position. It's fast and furious. You'll experience bumps, sharp bends and dirty tricks. While other books will focus on the banana skins and what might go wrong, BRILLIANT TEENAGER focuses you on the power-ups. What are they, where are they, and how can you use them to your advantage?

The aim is to challenge, entertain and inspire. BRILLIANT TEENAGER has depth, breadth and silliness. If it makes you think, ponder, question and laugh, that's great. If you maybe cry a little, even better.

It's your book so please own it. I want you to engage with it. If I ever pop round to yours for tea and cake and this book is sitting on your shelf in mint condition, I'll be heart-broken!

I want BRILLIANT TEENAGER to have coffee stains, Post-it Notes and folded-over corners. Basically, the tattier and more dog-eared, the better.

I want BRILLIANT TEENAGER to feel more like a journal than a book, so please get stuck in; scribble, draw, doodle, ponder... use the book like a spiritual windscreen wiper.

Life can feel heavy, which is why I've given BRILLIANT TEENAGER a deliberately light touch. I figure you need something to brighten your day, to challenge your thinking and to put a spring in your step. Please don't mistake my light touch for the book being lightweight. It's crammed with science, heavily disguised as common sense and fun.

Pressures of the world

Filthy rich

Putting myself in your shoes, I'm guessing you have two BIG questions and a demand:

How the heck am I supposed to be brilliant when I'm weighed down by the pressures of the world?

How is it that I don't ask much of life yet life keeps asking so much of me?

and your demand:

I want a signed apology from the world for the way it's been treating people. Including me!

The harsh reality is that the world doesn't care how you feel. If your plan is to sit patiently and wait for an apology, you'll die waiting. It's the same with success.

'Sitting patiently' is passive.

Talk is cheap.

> ## A little less conversation and a little more action.
> Elvis Presley
> (Film star and the 'King of Rock and Roll')

This book will challenge you to get off your backside and get busy doing something meaningful. But there's something a million times more important than what you're doing, and that's *who you're being.* This is where BRILLIANT TEENAGER is different.

Radically different!

It challenges you to do more and BE more.

The world needs YOU at your BEST.

The rest of this book is about how.

YOU

At your BEST

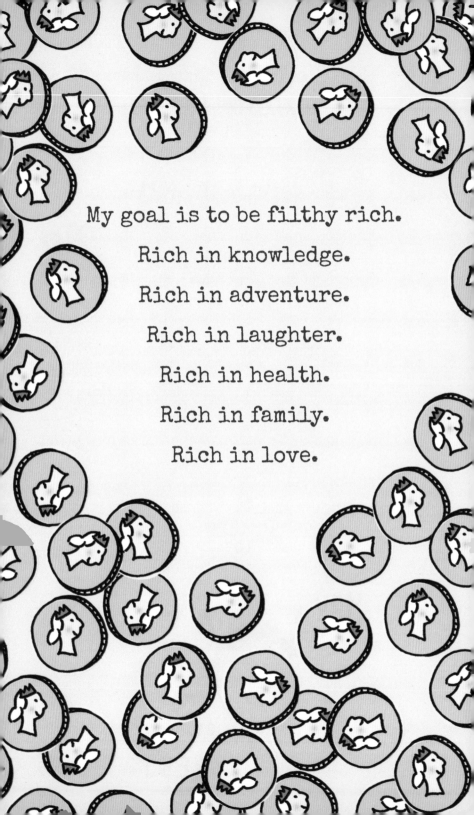

My goal is to be filthy rich.

Rich in knowledge.

Rich in adventure.

Rich in laughter.

Rich in health.

Rich in family.

Rich in love.

wake up
be amazing
be kind
be brave
be you

·repeat·

The facts of life

With fake news making the news, I've decided to throw some truths your way.

Here's your first fact of life. It's something they won't teach you in science even though it's actually one of the rules of the universe: *the harder you work, the luckier you'll get.*

Yes, I know, there's a piece of you saying, 'I might win the lottery.' If your life strategy is based on winning the lottery, your life will be very sad indeed. To save you a lifetime of hurt and disappointment, take it from me, you don't need a lottery ticket or scratch card, you need a better strategy.

TYPICAL! Nothing good ever happened to Miley. She enrolled for a class in 'Dealing with Disappointment' but the teacher never showed up

you are your biggest commitment

If you want to get super-lucky you need to work hard at school, and on yourself. **Note**, I didn't say you have to be hard on yourself, I said you have to *work hard* on yourself. You have to put effort into crafting a better you because here's a particularly hard-hitting fact of life: only a few fulfil their potential. Too many people condemn themselves to a life sentence of boredom and under-achievement.

So how do you become one of the few who are truly living their best life?

School's a great place to win some power-ups. There's nowhere better for history, art, science, maths and learning about dinosaurs. I'm absolutely *not* knocking school. If you want to earn more, *learn more*. I'm all for that!

But there's an awful lot of school stuff that's been useless in my adult life. For example, nobody's ever - I repeat never EVER - asked me to work out the area of a parallelogram or know the chemical reactivity of elements in relation to their position in the Periodic Table.

It would have been more useful to have lessons in why, periodically, I feel flat for no reason. How to bounce back from disappointment, regret and adversity - these are skills I've needed every single day!

At school we read a cracking love story called *Romeo and Juliet,* but my teacher never taught me how to love. Or how to be loved. Or what is love, actually?

A confusing English lesson...

'I' before 'e' except after
'Old MacDonald had a farm' ...

My PE teacher spoke about having a fire in my belly but what exactly did he mean. Where was the fire? How did it get there? And what if it goes out?

There were no lessons on how to repair a broken heart or how to make friends or how to maintain my enthusiasm for life when the world gets really tough. I had a massive argument with my bestie over something oh so silly. School never taught me how to say sorry (which I was), like I actually meant it (which I did).

I learned a foreign language but was never taught how to deal with the voice in my own head; how to live with nagging self-doubt and worry.

School will push you to work hard, meet deadlines and pass exams. It teaches you to *do* more, but never how to *be* more. And the biggest missing link is that nobody - not at school, college or in life - ever teaches you how to love and respect yourself, how to build mental strength that doesn't shrivel up when the world throws banana skins in your path.

Which, just so you know, it absolutely will!

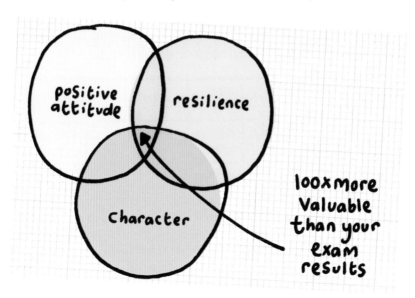

positive attitude

resilience

Character

100x more Valuable than your exam results

School is epic. Or, at least, it should be. If it's not, you're doing it wrong! You are built for learning, so please throw yourself into your lessons wholeheartedly. Soak it up but understand that school and life are different. In school, you're taught a lesson and then given a test. In life, you're given a test that teaches you a lesson.

So here's a test that life throws at you every day - a feeling of low-level dreariness. Nobody feels amazing all of the time (except your dog, right?). Sure, amazingness exists but it's mixed in with a big complicated mess of compassion, love, burden, fear, shame, sympathy, guilt, embarrassment, confusion, responsibility, joy, jealousy, overwhelm, frustration, uncertainty and anger.

So if you're feeling any of the above, relax, *you're perfectly normal*. A life well lived means you've experienced every single emotion. The trick is to learn to experience more of the amazing feelings and fewer of the less amazing ones.

DOG'S DIARY

BEST day of my life	BEST day of my life	BEST day of my life	BEST day of my life	BEST day of my life	BEST day of my life	BEST day of my life
BEST day of my life	BEST day of my life	BEST day of my life	BEST day of my life	BEST day of my life	BEST day of my life	BEST day of my life
BEST day of my life	BEST day of my life	BEST day of my life	BEST day of my life	BEST day of my life	BEST day of my life	BEST day of my life
BEST day of my life	BEST day of my life	BEST day of my life	BEST day of my life	BEST day of my life	BEST day of my life	BEST day of my life
BEST day of my life	BEST day of my life	BEST day of my life				

Another fact of life is this - you will mess up. The technical term for it is called 'being human'. For now, all you need to know is that just because you have messed up doesn't mean you *are* messed up. Bad stuff will surely feel bad. But it's part of the journey. If you want to feel better about yourself, think about all the most amazing people in your life, and all the super-duper celebs who've achieved greatness - I guarantee they've messed up loads!

I'll round off with the two biggest truths of them all.

Firstly, this *is* your life. It's not a rehearsal. You're not practising at it. You don't get a do-over, so it makes sense to embrace the whole thing. Savour the good. Learn from the bad.

The final fact of life is this: both shall pass.

The small print

'Expecting the world to treat you fairly because you are good is like expecting the bull not to charge because you are a vegetarian.'

Dennis Wholey

(American TV host and author)

Growing up, I had this sense that there was always some challenge or obstacle to be gotten through, and then my life would begin.

Until one day I realised these obstacles were my life. This changed everything. Instead of rolling my eyes and grumbling that 'life's not fair', I realised that nobody ever said it was. Life's not *supposed* to be fair.

I'm guessing if you had a contract for LIFE, it'd probably say something like this. Have a read, get a pen, sign on the dotted line, and I'll see you for a lovely story in part 2.

LIFE: The small print

Available for a limited time only.
Limit 1 (one) per person.
Subject to change without notice.
Life can have downs as well as ups.
No warranty.
No refunds.
Banana skins guaranteed.
fairness not included.
Best before death.

Signature————————————
Start date ————————————

#BrilliantTeenager #MarioLife #BeMoreDog

Important note:

You must take care of
yourself in life before
you can take care of
anyone else.

~~Poodles~~
Doodles!

Story 2.

The Golden Buddha

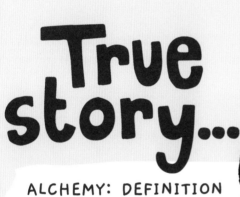

True story...

ALCHEMY: DEFINITION
The ancient science of turning base metals into gold.

Earlier this year I visited Thailand. In one of the temples sits a 5-metre-tall solid gold statue of Buddha, and next to the big bloke is a thick lump of clay. The two are linked, their story going back thousands of years...

The original gold statue was housed in an ancient monastery. The monks heard that robbers were planning to raid the monastery and steal the art and antiques, so they disguised the golden Buddha underneath a thick layer of clay. They figured that nobody would steal a pottery Buddha.

The good news is that the monks figured right. The golden Buddha was ignored but, bad news, all the monks were killed in the raid.

Hundreds of years passed and the monastery became overrun with jungle. Eventually a team of archaeologists chopped their way through the undergrowth and discovered the tumbledown monastery. They saw the giant clay Buddha and thought it would look good in their museum, so they tied ropes around the statue and tried to lift it onto their wagon.

But of course gold is super-heavy. The 'clay' Buddha actually weighed 6 tons, so the ropes broke and the statue fell to the floor, cracking the clay ever so slightly.

One of the team shone a torch and something glinted back at her. You've guessed it. They spent the next two days chipping off the clay to reveal the shiny statue in all its 24-carat glory. Today, the golden Buddha sits in Thailand's capital city and is reckoned to be worth millions.

It's more than a nice story. It points to a truth. If we're not careful we can all end up like the clay Buddha. We are amazing, but over the years we can get weighed down with negative thinking, self-doubt, pressure and responsibility. We learn how to fit in. We compromise. We go through the motions. We complain that life's not fair. We come alive at the weekends but go into our shell Monday to Friday.

Layer upon layer is added and we can end up losing our shine.

This story acts as a reminder that your brilliance is always there. BRILLIANT TEENAGER is about taking a chisel and chipping away at some of your 'clay':

Self-doubt: *that can go, for a start.*

Rolling your eyes and sighing: *may as well lose that habit too.*

Comparing yourself with others: *get rid.*

Counting down to the weekend: *why am I even doing that?*

Low-level grumbling: *it's a lazy habit; may as well bin it.*

Worrying about the past and stressing about the future: *life's too short for that nonsense.*

Thinking you're not good/clever/confident enough. *Let it go!*

Nothing *makes* us happy. We *are* happy. But it can get covered over by our thinking. If you continue to chip away at the stuff that weighs you down, you will reveal your shiny, world class, inner self. That's who you already are! Remember, you were born amazing. It's who you are meant to be. If you're not currently feeling it, it's not gone, just forgotten!

Oh, and the golden Buddha points us in one more important direction. There's gold in everyone else too. Spot it, call it out, bring out the best in others.

The bottom line is quite simple. You at your shiny best is one thing. Becoming a human alchemist is your gift to the world.

Get yourself some shades cos you'll need them.

Shine people, shine.

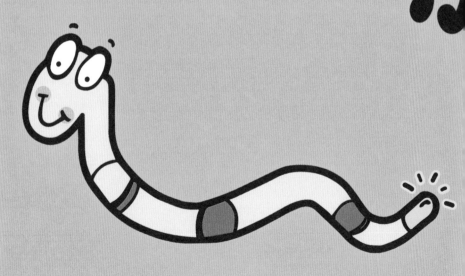

The Glow Worm Song

Secrets to living a long and fulfilling life:

♥ scroll half

♥ walk double ♥

♥♥♥ laugh triple

♥♥ love quadruple

Hm!

Lesson 3.

Dr Andy's marvellous medicine

True story: Melanie

When I was in primary school my teacher sat me next to a girl called Melanie.

Mel was really nice but at age 9 she developed a scowl and a bad attitude. She adopted a catchphrase that reflected exactly what she thought of school. Mel would slouch very low in her seat, roll her eyes and complain that everything was *'Boooooring'*.

And I mean 'everything' was out-loud *'Boooooring'*.

I remember the class taking turns reading pages from a story. I loved the story but when it was Mel's turn she huffed, 'What's the point of this story miss? *It's boooring.'*

'Numeracy is about numbers and they're *boooooring.'*

'History's just about dead people and it's *boooooring.'*

She'd peel the lid off her sandwich box and roll her eyes at the cheese sandwiches her mum had lovingly prepared! *'Boooooring!'*

You get the picture.

Then came the step up to big school. You've guessed it, Mel slouched her way through her teenage years complaining that big school was exactly the same as little school. *'Booooring.'*

Mel found her niche. She nestled into 'just below average'. Her default attitude was negative. Her exam results reflected her personality and I couldn't help feeling that Mel might have wasted an opportunity.

Flip it

That was four decades ago, so let's cut to today.

I'm a rotcod. That's 'doctor' backwards! I'm basically the exact opposite of all the other doctors you've ever met.

I'm not a medical doctor. I can't whip your appendix out, and please don't ask me to look at your rash or the fungus between your toes.

I'm a Doctor of Psychology. Most psychologists study mental disorders - anxiety, depression, phobias - those kinds of things. Once they've diagnosed you with something they can then set about fixing you.

That's all well and good but depression, anxiety, panic and stress... they're all skyrocketing. Despite the well-intentioned efforts of doctors, therapists and counsellors the truth is that mental ill health has actually been getting worse, not better. That's a big fat clue that what we're currently doing might need a re-think.

Way before you were born, I decided to do the exact opposite of what all the other psychologists had ever done. I decided to study happy people. My idea was this - what would happen if, for a change, instead of studying poorly people, we studied well people? So, instead of studying what's wrong with you, we studied what's right with you.

While the rest of the medical profession are crazy busy fixing people who need help, my starting point was a super-interesting counter-intuitive question: *who are the ones who aren't ill?*

Furrow that brow, put your learning face on, and let's get those brain cells buzzing. Here's some science...

If you asked a whole bunch of people how happy they are and plotted them onto a wellbeing graph (which is what I actually did) it'd look a little bit like this...

Happiness Chart

Much Happier Than Average

Most People MOST of The Time

Running On Empty

ALARM BELLS

2%ers
Perfectly fine
Negative mood
DANGER ZONE

Broadly speaking, if we measure levels of happiness and wellbeing on the lollipop chart, most people in the developed world inhabit the 'perfectly fine' zone. We generally have reasonable health, a roof over our head, a fridge full of food and a comfy bed. In terms of happiness, most people are 'mildly happy most of the time'.

BUT (and it's a big BUT), this millennium has seen change accelerate to warp speed. Climate emergency, social media, technology, algorithms, neurodiversity, gender fluidity, epidemics, pandemics, artificial intelligence, fake news, wars... in such challenging times, even those who were 'perfectly fine' have begun to run on empty, and before you know it, low-level negativity has kicked in.

People who've been running on negative thoughts for a long time can slip into the danger zone. This is where the mental health alarm bells begin to sound and, fingers crossed, the professionals will step in and offer therapy, counselling or meds. As I said a few paragraphs ago, this is how the medical profession has operated *forever*. They wait for people to be ill, and then step in to rescue them. That's noble, useful and absolutely the right thing to do.

BUT (and it's an even bigger BUT than last time) Positive Psychology is about those at the other end of the wellbeing spectrum - the handful of people that we can all think of who have something extra (positivity, energy, spring in their step, enthusiasm, passion for life...). I nickname them the 'two-percenters' on the basis that there aren't very many of them. The two-percenters spend more time towards the top end of the wellbeing graph and have been ignored by psychologists on the grounds of them 'not being ill'.

I flipped psychology on its head and came at it from the top end of the wellbeing graph. The happy outliers, the flourishing few, those who are genuinely living their best lives... I wanted to know 3 things:

1. The people who are feeling amazing on a regular basis, who the heck are they?

2. What are they doing that allows them to flourish?

3. What can we learn so we have a better chance of living our best life?

There are three pieces of good news about being a two-percenter. First, and most obviously, being your 'best self' more of the time will fundamentally change the rest of your life. Research suggests that happy people are more creative, motivated, energetic, healthy and connected. We all feel amazing sometimes. The trick is to feel amazing more often.

Second, research points to the fact that upgrading to 'best self' is actually a set of learned behaviours. The two-percenters are not feeling brilliant by accident. Their amazingness comes from a set of learned behaviours. There are simple principles that, when applied, will nudge you in the right direction.

Third, and best news of all, is that your wellbeing is bigger than you. Human emotions are contagious, so when you're functioning at your best, you create an emotional uplift in those around you. Sure, being a two-percenter is good for you, but it also spills out into your family, friends, teachers, neighbours and community.

your HAPPINESS is catchy!

Remember, you have been criticising yourself for years and it hasn't worked. TRY approving of yourself and see what happens.

Louise L. Hay

American author and motivational guru

But before I go any further, it might be worth stopping for a minute to reflect on you and your life. Concentrating on the positive end of the wellbeing graph - the two-percenters, the happy few, the ones who shine - who the heck are they?

Activity:
Who's who?

Who are the stand-out people in your life (not celebs, I'm asking you to think about family, friends, teachers, neighbours) and why do they stand out?

Now let's shift the focus to YOU! It's not big headed. It's not cringe. It might be uncomfortable but taking time to reflect on you at your best is the first step to getting there. Describe *yourself* in two-percenter mode. Be specific. What do you look, sound and feel like at your best?

boredom is the biggest disease in the world, darling

Freddie Mercury

ROCK STAR AND LARGER-THAN-LIFE CHARACTER

Cuddle, marry or avoid?

Oh, almost forgot. There's one more thing...

Picture the scene. I was in the supermarket. To be exact, I was in the fruit and vegetable section admiring the broccoli. I popped a bunch of the good stuff into my basket and as I looked up I caught the eye of a woman staring at me from the stir-fry section.

It was one of those uncomfortable moments where I felt I knew her from somewhere but I'm rubbish with faces and names so I shuffled onwards to the next thing on my list.

Oven chips. So much choice! I looked up from the freezer and there she was again, still staring at me! How rude! This time the woman cast a weak smile my way and started walking towards me.

She broke into a jog and held her arms out wide for a hug. She started squealing, 'Are you Andy?'

My mind clicked through its stored images. Mel? Could it really be Mel from school? After 30 years?

'Yes,' I nodded and we started running towards each other like the long lost lovers we never were. We met in a big cuddle at the crinkle cut chips.

'Gosh, is it you?' I asked.

'It iiiiis,' she squealed, her face reddening a little. *'It's meeee.* I saw you earlier. You know, next to the broccoli. And I thought it might be you Andy.'

I was delighted to see her. 'It must be 30 years?' I said, a huge grin lighting up my face.

'Nearly forty,' stated Mel proudly. 'I haven't seen you since we left school.'

'That's a heck of a long time,' I was so thrilled to meet an old school chum after nearly four decades, especially so randomly, at the supermarket. We'd shared all those lessons. We'd practically grown up together. 'Mel,' I said, 'how's your life turned out?'

And Mel rolled her eyes and sighed a huge sigh. 'Andy,' she said, 'it's turned out *booooring.'*

Know what? I've got a real problem with that story. My problem?

It's true!

It highlights the painful reality that underpins the entire book - *the habits that you get into now will stick with you for the rest of your life.*

Remember, Melanie was *boooring* at age 9 and she's booooring at age 59. But, good news, it also works in the opposite way; if you get into good habits NOW, those good habits will also stick with you forever.

Start today and continue every day because practice makes PERMANENT!

That's a pinkie promise!

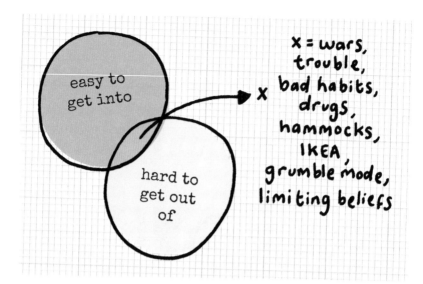

easy to get into

hard to get out of

x = wars, trouble, bad habits, drugs, hammocks, IKEA, grumble mode, limiting beliefs

YOU through and through

What 'trade mark behaviours' are you committing to? Behaviours that, if you apply day in and day out, will change your life for the better.

1

2

3

4

5

#BrilliantTeenager #Rotcod #TwoPercenter #PracticeMakesPermanent

Episode 4.

It's al<u>wa</u>ys choose-day

Future YOU!

CHILL

it's only chaos

Activity:
The school reunion

Twenty years from now you are going to meet up with your whole school year for a night of catching up, reflection and sharing what you have achieved in your life.

How old will you be in 20 years? Now imagine that you *are* that age. Write two accounts of that school reunion...

Imagine you've coasted for 20 years. You messed about at school and wasted your time. Basically, you couldn't really be bothered. You've carried that mediocre attitude around with you for two decades. At the school reunion you're going to have to chat about your life. What job are you doing? Who are you with? Where do you live? Describe your lifestyle. How do you feel? What do people say about you?

Now flip it and imagine you've been awesome for 20 years! You knuckled down at school and had a superb attitude. You've created opportunities and taken a few calculated risks. You're still learning, which means twenty years down the line you're doing well but there's plenty more success coming your way. You're really looking forward to catching up with your year group from back in the day. How has your life turned out? What job are you doing? Who are you with? Where do you live? Describe your lifestyle. How do you feel? What do people say about you?

20 whole years later!

Compare your potential lives. Both are possible.

TOP TIP:
choose the BEST one and live it.

love love love
LOVE Love love LOVE
LOVE love LOVE love
love
love LOVE
LOVE LOVE love
L♥VE love LOVE love love
love love LOVE love LOVE
love LOVE
love love love love
LOVE love LOVE

YOU 2.0

The biggest reason why most people are a million miles away from feeling brilliant is that it's *easier* to be negative. The bed of excuses is so warm and comfy, the finger of blame so easy to point and the unfairness of life so glaringly obvious.

Being yourself at your best requires effort. It's a learned behaviour. And because it's a bit harder and it takes practice, most people can't be bothered.

My message is quite simple:

GET BOTHERED!

Apologies for the shoutiness, but it's important! In fact, I can't think of anything more important that you'll ever learn to do. I promise that if you learn to be you at your best, and then do it for the next 80 years, it will change your life. No kid gloves here. I'm not messing. I'm not talking about it having a marginal effect around the edges of your existence. I'm telling you that being a two-percenter (and learning to stay there as often as possible) will fundamentally alter your life and spin you off into all sorts of exciting directions.

Oh, and in case you're wondering, I'm absolutely NOT talking about a new you. The awesome version of you already exists - it's you on a good day. It's the version of you before the world got its claws in.

A two-percenter is who you *really* are. You were born curious, questioning, with a thirst for learning. You were born for adventure. Pure potential. Pure love.

The world needs THAT version of you to step forward more of the time.

Happy Choose-Day

Who taught you this?

monday   Tuesday   Wednesday   Thursday   Friday

The question is HOW? How can I craft a truly amazing life? How can I create the best version of myself, especially when those around me seem okay to settle for mediocrity.

So here's the big reveal. The biggest thing that two-percenters do is also the simplest thing in the whole wide world (please imagine a drum roll...).

...They *choose* to be positive.

Let me say it again so the obviousness seeps into your bone marrow.

Those who are living their best life actually decide, every day, to tackle life with an attitude that works for them.

"A POSITIVE ATTITUDE may NOT solve all your problems BUT will annoy enough people to make it worth the EFFORT

Herm Albright
(German Guy, Good painter)

To be clear, choosing to have a positive attitude doesn't make homework disappear. It doesn't stop the rain. It doesn't make long division any easier. It doesn't mean you're guaranteed to win your next football match. No matter how positive you choose to be, adversity and unfairness will still exist.

What positivity does is put you in a better position to deal with the homework, rain, long division, a football match and adversity. Instead of stopping you in your tracks, these glitches are obstacles to be overcome. While everyone else is negative about the homework, grumbles about the rain, struggles with the long division carryovers and gets nervous before the match, your positivity shines through.

Choosing to carry an attitude that works *in your favour* is a monster power-up. And it's always choose-day!

Here are some positive choices that you can start making, right now:

Choose progress over perfection.

Choose courage over fear.

Choose responding positively over reacting negatively.

Choose losing and learning over winning and celebrating.

Choose optimism over pessimism.

Choose you over trying to be someone else.

Choose acceptance over judgement.

Choose hard work over an easy life.

Choose doing what's right over doing what's easiest.

Choose botheredness over can't-be-botheredness.

Choose kindness over meanness.

Choose Mondays over Fridays.

Choose giving it a go over giving up.

Choose personal responsibility over blaming others.

Choose opening your eyes rather than rolling your eyes.

But most of all, choose what this chapter's been all about...

The attitude you carry around with you will affect your entire day, so it pays to choose positive over negative.

It matters!

It *really* matters!

The 90/10 Principle

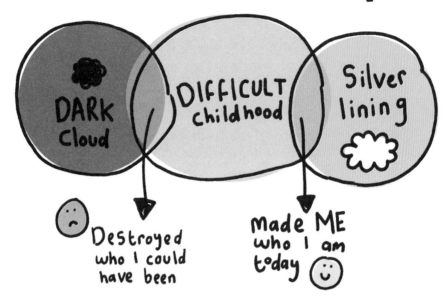

There are only two things you can truly be in control of:

1. Your preparation for what *might* happen.
2. Your *response* to what has just happened.

The universe is pretty much in control of everything else!

The 90/10 Principle preps you for both.

It suggests that 10% of whether you have a good day or a bad day is down to what happens to you. So, for example, your bus is late, or you're stuck in a queue at the supermarket, or you're camping in the rain, or you've got too much homework...

You can't control the 10% - 'life' happens to you every single day.

The 90/10 principle suggests that 90% of whether you have a good day or bad day is about how to choose to respond to the 10%.

So, basically, you can't control the late bus, the supermarket queue, the rain or the homework... they're going to happen whether you want them to or not.

90% of whether you have a good day or bad day is down to your *response* to these situations.

Your *attitude* is the 90%. That's massive!

Once you realise you can choose a better attitude, you'll find your day goes a whole lot better. Everyday events become so much easier to handle.

Homework - it's not ideal but the 90/10 Principle puts you in control. Instead of sitting looking at it, you attack it with some enthusiasm and it's done and dusted.

Camping in the rain - it's not the perfect situation - but rather than sitting in your tent grumbling about it being the worst holiday ever, you put your wellies on and go jumping in the puddles.

Your mum's shouting upstairs for you to get out of bed - the 10% tells you that you've got to get out of bed whether you like it or not. The 90% says you may as well attack the new day with some positivity.

In the three examples above, the exact same things are happening to you, but a different choice of attitude gets you a much better outcome.

The 90/10 principle boils down to this - that person in the bathroom mirror has a lot more control over your day than you think.

Subject 5.

The School of UN-Learning

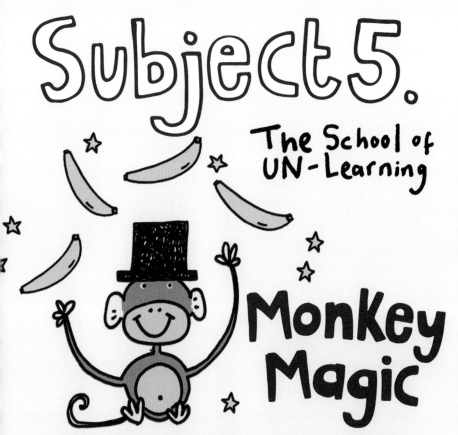

Monkey Magic

I'm thinking of setting up a school and calling it the SOUL Academy; The School of Un-Learning. Instead of cramming you with more knowledge and stress, it'd do the opposite. The lessons would peel back some of the un-truths and focus on *un-learning* the lies that you've accidentally picked up along the way.

There are thousands of fibs, but they tend to centre around one humongous un-truth:

I'm not enough.

To help peel away at the nonsense, here's a story that you'd read on day one of SOUL Academy. It's so powerful that once you've understood it you could have the rest of the week off.

How do you catch a baby monkey? Sounds like the start of a joke but read on, this is true.

First, to catch a monkey, you have to go to a place where monkeys live (i.e., the jungle) and dig a hole in the forest floor. You then fit a cage into the hole and place a banana in the cage. The monkey catcher then retreats behind a tree and waits.

Said primate will scamper through the forest, see the fruit and think, 'Yum yum, I like bananas.' Our furry friend will then reach in and grab the prize. But the cage has been cunningly designed so that once the primate makes a fist to grab the fruit, it can't get it's hand out through the bars.

Picture one bamboozled baboon, confused chimp or muddled macaque - its arm is in the cage, fruit grasped tightly - but it's unable to get the food into its mouth.

Once the primate has grabbed the banana, it's doomed. The monkey-catcher doesn't have to creep out, really quietly, and pounce on the animal. He or she can simply saunter up to the monkey, as loud as you like, and capture it. 'Gotcha! Lifetime in zoo for you.'

The creature can see the man approaching and knows it's going to get caught. Yikes! All it has to do is let go of the fruit and scamper away. But here's the rub, the monkey would rather hang on to the fruit and get captured, rather than let go.

This true story begs a really interesting metaphorical question - how many bananas do you have in your head? How many negative thoughts do you continue to think - thoughts that aren't serving you well - but you continue to think them anyway.

'I'm rubbish at so-and-so.'

'I'm sooo stupid.'

'I'm not confident enough.'

'I'm not clever enough.'

'I'm stuck.'

'I'll never be good at maths/English/PE/art/history/etc.'

Or, even worse, how many of those limiting thoughts turn into negative behaviours? You develop a set of habits that aren't working out for you, but you continue to do them...

Watching too much trashy TV.

Eating too much junk food.

Have an extra 30 minutes in bed rather than doing any exercise.

Walking with slumped shoulders instead of having a spring in your step.

Being grumpy in the mornings.

Showing up at school in average mode.

To live life as a two-percenter (i.e., to upgrade to 'best self' and stay there as often as possible) requires you to learn some good habits. Human beings are learning machines. We're really good at learning new things.

But here's something that other books never tell you, and it's something the School of UN-Learning would major on - to have an amazing life you also need to stop doing things that aren't working for you. Just as in the monkey story, we all need to let go, but guess what? Human beings are really bad at un-learning. It's much harder to stop your bad habits of thinking and behaving than it is to learn new ones.

Which points to a startling realisation... the biggest thing stopping you being brilliant is YOU! If you want to take giant leaps towards your potential you have to get out of your own way.

Of course, it's almost impossible to let go of a belief you don't know you have. That sentence sounds odd, but our personal 'bananas' are so ingrained that, often, they've become such a part of you, so entrenched, that you're not aware that you've made them up. So, identifying what your metaphorical bananas are is actually a great starting point.

Think about it. What do you keep saying or doing that is holding you back?

Drop the bananas!

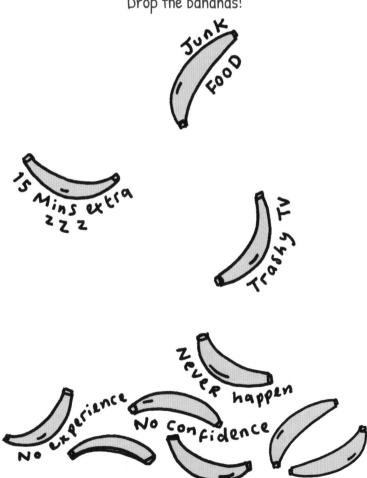

Permission to shine

It's difficult to but a price on the value of this page. It's a permission slip that allows you to let go of your bananas. Think of it like a Get Out of Jail Free card, which stops you getting into jail in the first place.

Your permission slip is valid for the rest of your life and you can use it as often as you want. All you have to do is sign it and remember to use it when you need it.

Permission Slip

I,

[PLEASE PRINT YOUR NAME HERE]

....,

hereby give myself permission to be awesome. I will not be embarrassed to be stand-out amazing. Instead, I will shine and let others catch the glow.

From this day forward, I'm granting myself permission to change what needs changing. I empower myself to love and be loved. I will pat myself on the back when I've earned it, forgive myself when I mess up and allow myself to ask for help when I need it. I have my consent to let go of negative thinking and habits that might be holding me back.

I don't need anyone else's approval, I need mine. Therefore, I am handing responsibility for my future to me. I am in agreement with myself to raise my personal bar, go for my dreams and to give life a right good go.

I acknowledge that life will not roll out the red carpet for me. I am in charge of the choices I make and the effort required. I am granting myself permission to get excited about doing the heavy lifting that will be needed to craft the life that I want.

The 'I am not enough' mantra is actually true. The fact is that I'm waaaaaay more than enough. I'm a one-in-eight-billion miracle. That's why I'm in agreement with myself to quit playing small. No more waiting. Starting now, I have the personal stamp of approval to BE myself and to LIKE myself. Not on an over-the-top sickly self-love way, but in a quietly confident 'I've got this' way.

It might not be easy, but it'll be worth it. Best life, I'm coming at ya!

Love,

Me

[PLEASE SIGN YOUR NAME HERE]

. . . .

Date . . . .

#BrilliantTeenager #SOULacademy #DropTheBanana
#PermissionSlip

Take a moment to be proud of yourself for surviving the days that felt impossible

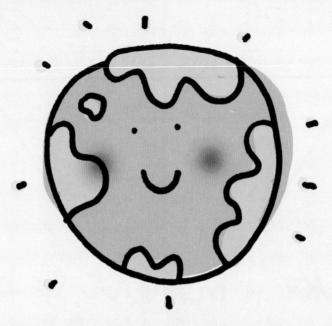

The twelve best doctors in the world.

1. Outdoors

2. Rest

3. Exercise

4. Healthy diet (but with occasional cake)

5. Self-confidence   ↖ mmm cake!

6. Friendship

7. Good quality sleep

8. Happiness

9. Love

10. Time

11. Play

12. Not taking yourself too seriously

Theme 6.

Bouncebackability.

Rolling
with life's punches

Ordinary magic

I'm a lot older than you so I can look back at life with something called hindsight. My first few decades were characterised by a lack of self-belief. My biggest challenge was this – *how on earth am I going to get others to believe in me when I can't even recruit myself?*

I want to share loads of learning with you, but my hindsight starts with bad news. You won't stop worrying you're not enough, and the world's not going to bend over backwards to make you happy. You won't stop getting hurt and, guess what, bad stuff happens to good people.

And while most books will expand on what mental toughness is, it's worth reflecting on what it absolutely isn't. Mental toughness is not about pretending things are okay when they're not. Neither is it about suppressing negative feelings, or hiding them.

There are times in everyone's lives when the normal rough and tumble of life becomes a bit brutal.

That's why resilience is super-important.

Everyone knows that your physical body is resilient. It's self-repairing. Think about it - if you cut yourself, it bleeds, then scabs over, starts itching and when the scab falls off, there's a brand-new piece of you underneath.

What most people don't realise is that emotions work on the same self-healing principle. We all possess what's called 'ordinary magic'. When bad stuff happens, *ouch* does it hurt. Worse than a broken leg. For example, when you pluck up the courage to ask someone out and they say 'no', the embarrassment stings! Trust me, that takes a while to get over.

Or, much worse than that, someone you love passes away, or the love of your life ditches you. These are heart-breaking moments. I'd be amazed if you manage to navigate growing up without episodes of anxiety, tears, fall-outs and emotional outbursts. Having a meltdown is actually par for the course. If you want one, go ahead and have one! Know what? Adults have meltdowns too!

So please be assured that if you are occasionally sobbing because someone's upset you or you are overwhelmed by the mere fact of growing up, it's not a sign that you're mentally unhealthy. An occasional meltdown is a sign that you're learning to experience intense emotions. Over time, you begin to master them. That's how it works.

Take it from me - sometimes there's no alternative but to sit down and have a huge sob. Crying serves a purpose. It lets stuff out. It shows the world you're hurt. Tears are the start of the repairing process.

It's messy, but crying is your safety valve.

#CheckMate

There are times when you're perfectly within your rights to feel sorry for yourself. My friend Professor Paul McGee[1] suggests that humans should learn a lesson from hippos. From time to time, we all need a good wallow.

So #BeMoreHippo. Have a bad day. *Enjoy* your wallow! Hippo Time is a necessary and important part of your journey, but please take a moment to digest the Prof's next point...

Wallowing is *not* your final destination. You've got to find the courage to haul yourself out of the swamp. Mental strength is about getting back in the game. It's about having a positive mindset, learning from failure, making good choices (*consistently*) and spending your energy wisely.

It's worth reminding you of this – sometimes the bravest thing you will ever do is ask for help. If you think about it, asking for help is a sign of remarkable courage. It's a signal that you're refusing to give up.

---

[1] Paul's book is well worth a read. *Yesss!: The SUMO Secrets to Being a Positive, Confident Teenager.*

Check on your mates

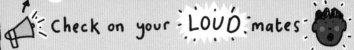 Check on your LOUD mates

Check on your quiet mates

 Check on your 'always OK' mate ok!

Check on your **grumbly** mate

 Check on your **SICK** mate Check on your healthy mate

 Check on your SCHOOL mate

 Check on your team mate

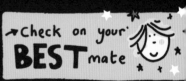 Check on your **BEST** mate

Check on yourself, mate
#checkmate

'Sometimes you're
the windshield;

Sometimes you're
the bug.'

MARK KNOPFLER (ROCK STAR)

All the way from Finland

I've noticed something. There are a lot of giver-uppers. When things don't go their way, too many people are too quick to wave the white flag.

Which is why I'm bringing you a word all the way from Finland. *SISU* (pronounced see-soo) is the psychological strength that allows a person to overcome extraordinary challenges. *Sisu* is similar to what we might call perseverance, or grit. It's your reserve tank, something you tap into when you're running on empty. *Sisu* is about digging deeper than you thought you could dig. It's about determination, bravery and a willingness to keep going even when you feel like giving up.

You might need to find extra reserves of energy for the last ten minutes of your football match, or extra confidence for an audition, or just to hang in there when your maths teacher is droning on, and on, and on, and on about equations. But *sisu* runs much deeper than that. It's about hanging in there during the worst of times.

Sisu, ordinary magic, grit, bravery, resilience, digging deep... there's a certain boldness about being able to stare difficult situations in the face and yet somehow keep moving forward. It's actually quite heroic.

Here's how to find your *sisu*...

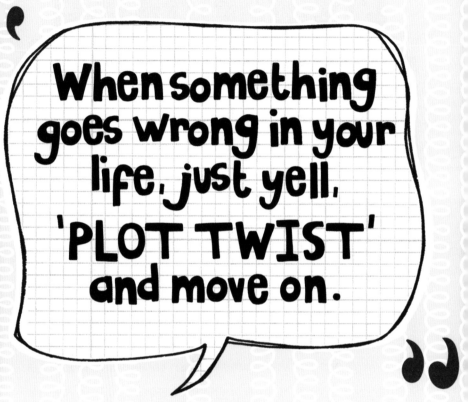

When something goes wrong in your life, just yell, 'PLOT TWIST' and move on.

GAVIN OATTES.
Scottish comedian, author
and all-round good guy

Tales of the unexpected

You are a story teller. Not just you, all humans are. Stories are what link us to our ancestors and to those who don't yet exist. Your inner story is one of the great classics, although only in your own head.

So my advice is to change your story. When things don't turn out as you expected, instead of 'disaster', 'problem', 'nightmare' or 'it's not fair' I'd like you to start calling them 'plot twists.'

In fact, don't just think or say it, shout it out. *Rejoice!* All the greatest books and movies have a plot twist, an unexpected turn of events that nobody saw coming.

In fact, imagine the opposite. Imagine a book or movie with no plot twists...

Darth Vader isn't Luke Skywalker's dad. In actual fact, it turns out that Luke's dad is Henry Skywalker, an accountant who gets a kick out of attending virtual meetings.

Charlie Bucket unwraps the chocolate bar and there is no golden ticket so he scrolls on his phone instead.

Harry Potter is just a 10-year-old kid with a scar on his forehead that he got from falling off his skateboard. The end!

How painfully predictable and utterly dull!

A life is not an amazing life without plot twists. Ups and downs. Twists and turns. The turbulence, challenges, strains, sadness, disasters and happy moments.

You're a young person. The story of your life has only just begun. There are plenty of story lines left to write and numerous plot twists still to play out. There's ample time to create a juicy middle and a happy ever after.

So I want you to rewrite your story. You're not a victim, imposter or a baddie. You are not a nobody - you are very much a *somebody*. You are the A-lister in the story of your life. There are no disasters or nightmares, just a few unexpected plot twists.

I want you to write yourself into your life as the heroic central character.

Activity:
Read all about it!

Imagine you are 80 years old and you've achieved some amazing things. The news channel has picked you out to feature on its 'local heroes' website.

What would you like the headline to be?

_____

_____

_____

_____

_____

Write the story. What plot twists came your way, what personal battles have you won, what have you made happen in your life, what are people saying about you, what quote would you give the newspaper reporter?

The magic words

Here are 7 words that changed my life. It doesn't sound like a life-changing sentence, but I promise you, it is.

Do it better than you have to.

And by 'it' I mean 'everything'.

Put more effort in than you have to.

Put your hand up and volunteer an answer a bit more often than you have to.

Use your manners better than you have to.

Be a better learner than you have to.

Eat your veggies a bit better than you have to.

Help around the house a bit better than you have to.

Play with your annoying little sister/brother a bit better than you have to.

Do your homework a bit better than you have to.

Do better handwriting than you have to.

Be a better friend than you have to.

... you get the point.

All these *little bit better than you have tos* add up to the difference between YOU 1.0 and YOU 2.0. It's not about making dramatic changes. I'm suggesting you start doing lots of little things a bit better than you did them yesterday. And tomorrow, a teensy weensy bit better again.

And again.

And again.

And again.

And again.

And again...

It's about small improvements in attitude and behaviour every single day. I think you'll really enjoy the upgrade and, guess what, these changes start to become normal, they get grooved into your habits and, hey presto, there's an everyday superhero staring back at you while you brush your teeth.

Rise above mediocrity by doing
everything a little bit better
than you have to. Remember,
there's hardly any traffic
on the extra mile.

#BrilliantTeenager #Bouncebackability #OrdinaryMagic
#CheckMate #Sisu #PlotTwist

" Your future hasn't been
written yet. No one's has.
Your future is whatever
you make it. So make it a
good one. "

Doc Brown, *Back to the Future*

Idea 7.

FIVE Seconds that will change your life[2]

Bouncing forward

TOP TIP:

Conventional wisdom suggests that if you're angry you should 'count to 10' which allows the red mist to evaporate.

Research suggests that it actually takes about 20 minutes for anger to work through your system. So, top emotional intelligence tip, don't count to 10 when you're mad, count to 1,200!

Bouncing back is one thing. Bouncing *forward* is next level. This is when adversity strikes but you come back stronger.

Here's something that helps me find the courage to BE confident, resilient and brave. It's called the 5-second rule and it literally kickstarts me into action.

---

[2] Thank you, Mel Robbins.

Sometimes the alarm goes and I really don't feel like getting out of bed. Especially when it's dark outside and I have things to do that don't excite me.

It's easier to stay in bed an extra half an hour. But my extra 30 minutes in bed means I start the day late and I'm playing catch-up all day, rushed, stressed, on edge and angry with myself.

On those mornings when my mojo has slipped, instead of rolling over and going back to sleep I do the 5-second rule...

I count down - 5, 4, 3, 2, 1 - and launch myself out of bed.

> **Friend, the comfort zone is holding you back.**
>
> Christian Bosse
>
> American author and poet

It works because your brain is very good at finding excuses for you NOT to do things. Humans are the animal kingdom's best over-thinkers. The longer you leave it before taking action (the longer the gap of over-thinking time), the more likely it is that the gap gets filled with dread, anxiety, self-doubt and negativity, or good old-fashioned things called EXCUSES.

In my 'getting out of bed' example, if I think about it for too long my brain will come up with lots of reasons why staying in bed is the best option. My thinking is exactly like your thinking, it can be very convincing... *it's so warm and snuggly in here and, besides, an extra half an hour won't hurt. In fact, it might do me good. And I can skip breakfast... I mean, who needs breakfast anyway, it's so over-rated...* and before I know it, I've nodded off and I'm running late, 'hangry' and stressed.

The 5-second rule cuts the thinking gap. The alarm goes and *5, 4, 3, 2, 1 BOOM!* I'm out of bed and ready for action. Feet planted, sleep wiped from my eyes and my brain is like, 'Wow, no messin'. You mean ACTION today'.

It's not just about waking up in the morning, the 5-second rule will work for you in all sorts of everyday situations:

Your mum's asked you to switch off the computer game and sort your homework out: *5, 4, 3, 2, 1...* you're sitting at the kitchen table and getting to work. Best of all, your family is argument free.

Auditions for the school play and you're not sure if you should: *5, 4, 3, 2, 1...* the lead role is yours!

You should be going to rugby practice but it's drizzling so you're not sure if you can be bothered: *5, 4, 3, 2, 1...* you're out of the door, enjoying the drizzle and the player of the season trophy is yours.

There's an amazing human being in your life and you're not brave enough to go talk to them: *5, 4, 3, 2, 1...* 'Hi there, I'm xxxx. I'm loving your trainers. Where did you get them from?'

tomorrow

(noun)

A mystical land where 99% of all human productivity, motivation and achievement is stored.

Remember, your brain is brilliant at inventing all sorts of wonderful excuses (too tired, scared, busy, unwell, stressed, not ready) that make perfect sense.

So don't let it!

Otherwise we put it off... and we put it off... and we put it off... and opportunities pass us by.

The 5-second rule is an accelerator, but it also works as a brake. It can stop you doing rubbish things.

You sit staring at your homework. It stares back. You're not in the mood and are about to log on to YouTube instead: 5, 4, 3, 2, 1... you've made a positive start and 30 minutes later you've smashed it.

About to post a negative message on social media: 5, 4, 3, 2, 1... you've changed it to a nice message.

About to guzzle a can of sugary fizz: 5, 4, 3, 2, 1... 'Actually can I have a glass of water instead please?'

About to open a packet of biscuits and scoff the lot: 5, 4, 3, 2, 1... you've reached for a piece of fruit instead.

The 5-second rule is simple, free and quick. Best of all, the 5-second rule puts YOU in the driver's seat of your own life.

5, 4, 3, 2, 1- take one action - and you will have freed yourself from the shackles of your comfort zone. You will become a ninja of action. You will be streets ahead of those who are making excuse after excuse after excuse after excuse after excuse.

After excuse...

... after excuse.

The 5-second rule will break you out of your comfort zone into your stretch zone. This is important because it's a little known truth that people who live in comfort zones are actually very uncomfortable.

Yes, 'comfort zone' and 'regret bubble' are two sides of the same coin.

I've left you some space to reflect on your own examples of where you can apply the 5-second rule. One last tip: use the 5-second rule quietly, in your head, otherwise people might think you're a bit strange!

your Puny
comfort zone

10 situations where I can use the 5-second rule:

1.

2.

3.

4.

5.

6.

7.

8.

9.

10.

'Money can buy you a fine dog, but only LOVE can make him wag his tail.'

Kinky Friedman. American singer, songwriter and politician.

Humans are all made of flesh and blood, with emotions, dreams, hopes, fears and insecurities. We're built to certain specifications so are able to withstand the normal wear and tear of life, but remember, the pressures of the modern world are considerable.

People do actually break - and that's fine. It's to be expected. Your family and friends don't come with a receipt. If they're wilting under the strain, or if they have developed a fault, or have actually broken, you can't take them back to the shop and swap them for a new one.

But here's a sure-fire 100% guaranteed way to help fix a broken friend or parent.

You must put the love back into their hearts.

First, if it was you who caused them to break, say sorry and mean it. That will help you and them to move on and put whatever 'it' was behind you. And that's where you need to leave all your troubles - in the past.

Second, if it wasn't you that caused them to be on a downer, it was just 'life' generally, tell them you love them and mean it.

The third thing in your love repair kit is to administer a magical 7-second hug. Note, the average hug lasts 2.1 seconds so 7 seconds is really stretching it. Which is exactly the point. Sometimes your loved ones need a pick-me-up so a 7-second hug, plus an 'I love you' and/or 'I'm sorry and I mean it' is a wonderful explosion of genuine affection. It heals almost anything.

If you don't believe me, put the book down, go do a 7-second hug, and report back.

HUG DEALER

Hug Dealer small print

Seven seconds is an I ♥ U hug. No words are necessary. Seven seconds is just long enough for the other person to know that you love them. It contains life-changing properties but should only be administered to very close family and friends. It's absolutely NOT for strangers in the park because that would be weird. Never count out loud because it spoils the effect. You don't actually have to wait for your siblings, parents, gran or bestie to look jaded before you do the 7-second hug thing. They provide an instant boost pretty much anytime. Warning: 7 seconds is advanced hugging. Those who are already huggy will absolutely love the full 7 seconds but you'll be able to spot the non-huggers - they start wriggling and you have to cling on for the love to transfer. Good luck!

Discussion 8.

How to be an influencer

Jot down the top 10 happiest moments of your life. Go ahead and give it a go. I'll refer back to it in a minute:

1

2

3

4

5

6

7

8

9

10

The happiness formula

The boffins at University College London spent a load of time and money researching the secrets of happiness and, guess what, they did exactly what you'd expect scientists to do, they created a formula.

You ready for it?

Please imagine a drum roll.... while I reveal what humans have been searching for since time began - the secret formula for happiness, according to UCL

....is this....

$$Happiness(t) = w_0 + w_1 \sum_{j=1}^{t} y^{t-j} CR_j + w_2 \sum_{j=1}^{t} y^{t-j} EV_j + w_3 \sum_{j=1}^{t} y^{t-j} RPE_j$$
$$+ w_4 \sum_{j=1}^{t} y^{t-j} Max(R_j - O_j, 0) + w_5 \sum_{j=1}^{t} Max(O_j - R_j, 0)$$

How utterly rubbish is that!

If you unpick the formula it basically suggests that you should lower your expectations of happiness, and that way, you'll never be disappointed.

I have several issues with the formula. First, they seem to have confused it with rocket science; second, it's wrong (why on earth would you go through life with such low expectations?); and third, the secret of happiness doesn't require a complicated formula at all.

If you look at all the positive psychology research that's ever been done and do what's called a meta-analysis (that means you analyse lots of analysis), you'll discover that the secret of happiness is in fact…

Relationships!

So, yes, the weather, money, purpose, attitude and gratitude all play a part in your happiness pie, but the biggest slice is people. More specifically, your ability to belong to a team, tribe, clan, community or family.

If you revisit your top 10 happiest moments from the previous activity list, I'm almost certain that there won't be any products there. Your happiest moments will be experiences, with people you love.

Happiness = Experiences + People; that's the happiness formula right there!

The Secret

Plot spoiler, what goes around comes around, so be a giver, not a taker.

If you want more happiness, *be* happy.

If you want more kindness, *be* kind.

If you want love, *be* lovable.

If you want friendship, *be* a good friend.

If people don't understand you, take steps to understand them *first*.

If people aren't nice, try being nice to them *first*.

I promise that if you're consistently awesome, the world is a better place. It's a bit spooky how true this is.

However, just because you upgrade to 'amazing human being' it doesn't mean everybody is always nice and smiley and kind to you. The world will still have its fair share of idiots. Always remember, you can't cure stupid. Just make sure you don't become one of the idiots. Remember, when you shine, you stand out. And when you stand out, opportunities come your way

But here's the thing. You at your best is something to behold, but there's something even bigger than you, it's called 'family'. And there's something even bigger than family, it's called 'society'. And there's something even bigger than society, it's called 'humanity'.

So, if you want to do your bit for humanity, here's how...

how amaZZ-zZing
you sometimes
feel

how amaZZZZing
you really
ARE!!

Emotional soup

Our amazing human brains give us huge processing power but they are also constructed to *transfer* emotions. At its simplest level, someone smiles because they feel happy – you mimic the smile and also feel happy.

Basically, *you are contagious!*

Emotional contagion helps us build communities and relationships; love, empathy, happiness; these bind us together. In fact, I'll go further than that. The absolute truth is that you cannot NOT have an emotional impact on those around you.

It is truly a case of leading by example. If your attitudes and behaviours are infectious I guess the billion-dollar questions are: who will you 'emotionally infect' and what will you 'infect' them with?

Which brings me on to family and school. To make my point, it's helpful to think of any social situation as a soup – an *emotional soup* – in which everyone is adding some sort of 'flavour'. Take your family situation as an example. When you're all together, everyone is having a say in whether the family atmosphere is working. *Or not!*

So you need to consider what flavours you're adding to your family soup. Are you coming through the door with joy and enthusiasm or are you poisoning the family atmosphere with toxicity?

And second, not all family members are equal. Yes, everyone is adding something to the emotional soup but I've just read a research article that says... wait for it...*a teenager has the BIGGEST say in the atmosphere at home!*

Oh my goshness! YOU are the main ingredient!

It boils down to this: emotional leakage means a teenager having a good day is a joy to behold. You will light up your classroom, friendship group and family.

And, *ahem*, a teenager having a bad day... it hardly bears thinking about. Your toxicity is like secondhand cigarette smoke. You are negatively impacting on everyone you meet.

Suffice to say that the attitude you choose doesn't only have the power to make or break *your* day, but it also affects those closest to you.

Please wield it with the greatest of care.

Attitude is infectious...
is yours worth catching today?

"You are one in over 7.4 billion humans on this planet and although you might not be able to change the whole world, you can make a few of those worlds a tiny bit brighter."

Emily Coxhead
British designer and illustrator

Side effects

I was delivering our world famous 'Brilliant Schools' programme for a bunch of 14-year-olds in middle England and we got chatting about careers. Some of the teenagers were gunning for jobs that didn't exist a few years ago. One was already making some money from gaming. There were a couple building a social media following, there was a geeky lad who was into crypto currency, and there was a girl who insisted she was going to be an influencer.

So I steered the discussion in that direction.

You see, we're all influencers.

I'll spare you the scientific backstory but trust me, when you're in best-self mode, there are some glorious side effects. You will experience better relationships, less stress levels, more passion and an increasing engagement with life. Your 'emotional spillage' creates a ripple effect that reaches 3 degrees of people removed from you, meaning you are affecting you friends, your friends' friends, and your friends' friends' friends.

Here are the important numbers: 16, 10 and 6. Let me demonstrate the emotional ripple effect via an example.

Imagine you've got a smile on your face and a positive attitude. Everyone you meet - family, friends, teachers - experiences an emotional uplift of 16%. You, on a good day, light up those closest to you by a minimum of 16%.

But it doesn't stop there.

Those 16% happier folks then pass on their happiness to everyone they encounter, raising their levels by 10%. So, for example, your teacher is 16% happier because you've had a stellar lesson. They go home to their family and everyone in their family is now 10% happier (you haven't met your teacher's family but it's your happiness they've caught).

But there's one more ripple to be had. Your teacher's partner pops out to the shop to get something for supper and, because they're 10% happier, they have a nice chat with the checkout assistant and that lady is now 6% happier.

All because *you* were in a good mood to begin with!

How many people do you come into direct contact with every single day? I've done the sums for you: deliberately guesstimating on the low side, let's assume you meet three people at home, 30 other teenagers in class, five people at lunch, a shop assistant and five random passers-by on the way home from school.

That's 44 people that you've come into direct contact with but, remember, the ripple effect reaches 3-degrees of people removed from you. So your first ripple has reached 44.

For the sake of simplicity, let's assume that the 44 you met also meet 44 people. So your emotional ripple has now reached 44 x 44. The second ripple has now been felt by 1,936 people.

And to complete your impact, let's assume those 1,936 people each interact with 44 others.

You might need to sit down for this next number! You will have had some sort of emotional impact on 85,184 people.

That's no ripple. You are the epicentre of a tsunami of emotion that is felt across your family, school and community. That is superhero influencer territory - you truly are doing your bit for humanity!

NOTE: I'm not trotting out these numbers to pressure you into sticking a stupid grin on your face and *pretending* everything's tickety-boo when it's not. Remember, bad days are inevitable.

I'm informing you of the emotional ripple effect for information only. It might stiffen your resolve. Once you understand how impactful you are it seems sensible to work hard at creating more positive days than negative ones. If you can't be bothered to carry a positive attitude for yourself, do it for the people you love!

And, just to cement the learning, there's an academic report that also suggests a happy friend makes you 25% happier, a happy brother or sister raises your happiness by 14% and a happy neighbour raises your happiness by a whopping 34%.

So I'll conclude this section with a plea for you to do your bit for humanity:

Be that friend.

Be that sister or brother.

Be that neighbour.

Proposal 9.
Shut up and listen!

How to be a relationship ninja

In Positive Psychology there's something called the Dunbar number. It means you spend about 40% of your time with between 6 and 8 people. These are your very close family and friends.

Your tribe.

Another big chunk of your time is spent with an additional, slightly wider circle of half a dozen. If I cut to the chase, it boils down to this – you spend about 60% of your time with a dozen or so people.

It's worth pausing and thinking about your tribe. Who are your closest dozen?

Celia loved her computer because all her friends lived in it

The science is clear. Although you might have 10,000 'friends' online - your wellbeing is much more likely to be linked to quality of your relationships with your closest dozen flesh and blood friends and family.

So it's worth giving you a few pointers about relationships and people.

I think many of us, if we slow down long enough to take a look at ourselves, don't give our relationships the time or attention necessary to keep them healthy and happy. We end up taking people for granted - especially those we love the most, which is strange.

Paradoxically, in our hyper-connected world, more and more people are finding it harder to take the time to simply be with somebody else for a while. I'm talking eye contact, earphones out, with an actual real person.

Anyone can listen. All you have to do is take your earphones out, look up from your screen and stop talking! But to be a black belt listener you have to be genuinely interested in other people. Yes, *genuinely!* I call it 'listening with fascination' and it's a fabulous skill to develop. Listening with fascination is about being interested and asking follow-up questions.

I promise that if you're *genuinely* interested in other people, they'll think you're more interesting. I know, that's weird, right? Because it seems as though the more you talk about yourself, the more interesting you'll seem.

But, no, I'm afraid not.

Think about it... all the people you really like are interested in you, right? Because, bingo, that's how it works.

Keep your questions positive. So instead of, 'How was your day?' try asking, 'What was the highlight of your day?' 'What's been the best thing about your day?' 'What's gone well today?'

And when they share the good stuff, follow up with the best question ever, the one that will make YOU seem more interesting, which is simply this; *Tell me more...'*

Then shush, listen and be *genuinely* interested. You have two ears and one mouth for a reason.

They're talking about you behind your back

Most people understand what paranoia means. It's the nagging feeling that people are talking about you behind your back. Gossiping most probably. Making horrible remarks. Saying bad things, no doubt.

That's what being paranoid means.

But I bet you didn't know there was an opposite to paranoia?

Which is pronoia... when people are saying *nice* things about you behind your back!

Imagine other people talking about you but saying how amazing you are, or how kind, or what a hard worker you are, or how proud they are.

Pronoia - two top tips spring from your new word. A relationship quick win is to say nice things about people, *behind their back.* To their face too, obviously, but there's something extra-special about saying nice things about people when they're not there. It seems to super-charge the niceness.

It's free and simple. Often, your nice comments will find their way back to the person you were talking about which makes them feel amazing.

Of course, it's very easy to slip into the opposite. It's easy to gossip, pick fault or say nasty things about people behind their back.

So don't!

You can also extend the exact same rules to your online relationships. Remember it's called social media, not *anti*-social media, so less doom scrolling, no nastiness online and stop feeding the trolls. Instead of horrible comments, just post good stuff: praise, encouragement, love, positivity, gratitude.

It won't stop other people being nasty, but you're not other people. You're you. It doesn't matter what they're doing, it *matters what you're doing.* So be a lover, not a hater.

Interesting question:

The internet makes it easy to say nasty things about people. Things that you'd NEVER say to their face.

Why would anyone do that?

The positivity ratio

To avoid your relationships sliding back to average I'm going to share one more bit of relationship science with you. It's called the Losada Line. If you Google it you'll find it's one of those things that's been proven and disproven and proven and disproven and batted around a few times, but I like it because it's simple, free and it works.

For relationships to survive, you should be three times more positive than you are negative. Note, the ratio is 3:1, not 3 to zero, so you can be grumbly and negative if you wish, but every time you say something negative or critical, you should balance it up with 3 positives.

That's 3 bits of praise, 3 bits of encouragement, 3 bits of good news, 3 thank yous, 3 catching people doing things well and telling them...

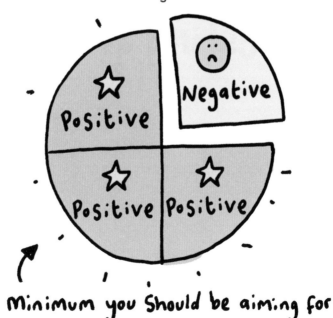

Minimum you should be aiming for

3:1 is the *minimum* you should be aiming for.

To create really strong buzzing relationships, your positive to negative ratio should be 6:1. That's 6 bits of praise, encouragement, good news, thanks, catching people doing good things and telling them. Six nice comments about people behind their back.

I'm not asking you to be stupidly positive and praise people for nothing. The 6:1 positivity ratio is about catching people doing little things really well, noticing, and letting them know you've noticed:

Great work

Thanks so much

That's amazingly kind

What a lovely smile

I love working in a group with you

Thanks for being on time

You've been so helpful

I love your positivity

I adore that scarf, where did you get it from?

Thanks Miss, for delivering such an interesting lesson. I loved it

Dad, you do the world's best fried eggs

If you cup your ear and listen you'll hear a lot of people doing the exact opposite. There will be 6 grumbles for every positive!

Remember, aiming to be your best self means you're setting a high bar. It'll be higher than those around you. Be honest. Listen back to yourself. If you want to create strong relationships six positives for every negative is the right ballpark to be in.

I always wondered why **somebody** didn't do something about that, then I realized **I am** somebody.

Challenge 10.

The missing 44 days

Some random phone stats[3]

- The average person looks at their phone 150 times a day. There's a category of super-users who glance at their beloved screen 358 times a day.

- 71% of people check their phone as soon as they wake up (3% of people sleep with their phone in their hand and 15% with it under their pillow).

- 64% of people use their phone on the toilet (and a third of them have dropped their phone down the toilet, some more than once).

- 61% of people have texted someone in the same room as them.

- 48% feel panic/anxiety when their phone battery dips below 20%.

- 36% would rather give up their pet than their phone.

- 66% of people show signs of nomophobia (smartphone addiction).

- 52% of teenagers sit around in silence, staring at their phones, when they are together with friends.

- 41% of teenagers feel overwhelmed by notifications on their device.

The average phone use is 2 hours and 54 minutes per day (which equals 44 days per year). NOTE, we average about 45 minutes of daily face-to-face contact with our families.

---

[3] Sources: techinjury.net, business insider, reviews.org

Top Kip tip zᶻᶻ

Waking up and checking your phone and social media is like letting 1,000 screaming people into your bedroom before you've even gotten out of bed. Peace smashed. Adrenaline primed. Grump mode activated.

To avoid such a rude awakening, leave your phone in the kitchen.

→ Could happen...

Civilisation collapses. Nobody looks up from their phones.

BIG thought about FOMO and screen time. The ultimate irony is that we absolutely are missing out. On the moment. THIS moment. Make yourself a priority. Treat yourself to phone detox. It's like kale for the mind.

Jill and Ted's Excellent Adventure

You were born into a world of screens. Your entire life has been filmed and shared by your mum and gran. You have a small hand-held device that enables you to access all the information in the entire world. It has apps that allow you to communicate, download, interact and share.

It's no wonder you look at it a lot!

Science and technology seem to have thought of everything, except how to make us all happy and contented. If I tell you to spend less time on your phone, or cut the time on your games console by 70%, you'll roll your eyes and ignore me. If I reel off some stats about the link between screen time and depression, it'll make no difference whatsoever.

So chill. I'm not going to lecture you. Instead, I'm going to credit you with enough intelligence to read and absorb the story of Jill and Ted. If you have a go at the activity that follows, some personal change might follow. Or it might not?

Who knows?

Sitting comfortably? Let me tell you about nine-year-old classmates Jill and Ted...

Both had a games console and both loved FIFA. Sometimes, in the evenings they'd log on and have a cheeky game or two. Or nineteen.

Then Miss Cleverclogs gave the class some homework. 'This week,' she announced, 'I want you all to log how many hours of screen time you do. No fibs. No ifs. No buts. No cheating. Every time you sit in front of a screen, you count the minutes and write them down.'

'All screens?' grumbled Bella. 'Like TV, iPad, laptop and everything?'

'All screens,' nodded Mrs C.

'Is a phone a screen?' asked Ravi.

'A phone does indeed have a screen Ravi,' assured the class teacher.

****

One week later, the results were in. Miss Cleverclogs drew a graph on the board and plotted everyone's hours on it.

Ted was top. His weekends were spent almost entirely on his games console, plus about two hours each school day, so he averaged out at four hours and 13 minutes screen time per day. Ted had never been top of anything so a place on the screen time leader board gave him a playground swagger.

But Jill's average daily screen time of three hours and two minutes per day bugged her. She wondered if it would actually be better to be at the bottom of the screen time league table. And then she wondered an even bigger wonder - what if she replaced her screen time of three hours and two minutes of imaginary football with three hours and two minutes of actual real football.

She got her calculator out and did some numbers.

3 hours and 2 minutes = 182 minutes. That's how many minutes of screen time I do in a day.

She then calculated her screen minutes per year, and then between now and age 20. She then converted that massive number into hours, then days...

Jill stared at the number; 461 (and a bit) days!

It seemed enormous so she worked the numbers again. Same result!

Between now and age 20 she was going to spend way more than an entire year staring at a screen.

Except, obviously, she wasn't. Because while Ted ploughed on with his screen time, Jill decided she'd spend 3 hours and 2 minutes, *every single day,* playing actual football. She started with some kickabouts with her dad. Then she roped in a few mates and they played in the park with jumpers as goal posts. Then she joined a team and went training twice a week, playing in a league on Saturdays and Sundays.

She got fitter and stronger and better. Sometimes it rained and nobody else fancied it so Jill played on her own, hammering a football against a wall - left foot, right foot - time after time, after time, after time, after time, after time...

... after time.

While Ted was sitting in his bedroom getting really good at pretend football, Jill was out in the fresh air getting really good at the real thing.

Day after day, after day, after day, Ted played on his console.

Day after day, after day, after day, Jill played for real.

For 461 (and a bit) days.

****

Ted was super-excited for his 21st birthday. The delivery van pulled up outside and the young man went to help unload the super-massive widescreen surround sound 3D 10G holographic TV. They lugged it upstairs to Ted's tiny bedroom and plugged it in.

'You little beauty,' he said as he logged on and downloaded the brand new game: FIFA41.

His expert thumbs did all the work. To be fair, although he'd developed a bit of a pizza belly and a biscuit double chin, his thumbs were super-fit. Yes, Ted definitely had the best thumbs in the neighbourhood.

Ted was going to pick the best team. He scrolled. Keeper, tick. Defenders, tick. Midfielders, tick.

There was a forward he absolutely had to have. A young player who was a regular at Barcelona and on the verge of playing for England. Great stats. Good goal scorer. Tidy tackler. Superb with both feet.

Jill's face appeared on the screen. Ted clicked. 'Gotcha, old buddy,' he said.

Sum it up

The Jill and Ted story is emotional blackmail. It's just a silly, made-up thing to make me guilty about spending so much time online. **True/False?** **Discuss.**

Calculate your weekly screen time. All screens! No fibs, ifs, buts or maybes.

What's your screen time per year?

What's your screen time over 10 years?

What's your screen time over the next 80 years?

If you halved it, what else could you learn or do in that time?

How might that learning or doing help you?

moment of Seemingly Spontaneous Success
'NOPE'
Crying
'YOU can't Do that'
CRITICISM
Cancelled DATES
Sad emails to MOM
QUITTING
JEALOUSY
'NO!'
'you're NOT famous enough TO BE famous'
Late NIGHTs EARLY mornings
LOSS OF FRIENDSHIPS (Then again, NEW ones gained)
RejecTioN x 1000 000 000
'Absolutely NOT'
Stupid amount of online research
Sleepless nights
zz
* Putting yourself out there *

Activity 11.

#VL4Victory

A way of living:

Be fearless in the pursuit of what sets your soul on fire.

The good, the bad and the airbrushed

If I think back to when I was a kid my teachers, parents, aunts and uncles all used to ask the same question: 'Andy, what do you want to be when you grow up?'

And I'm like 9, I've got literally no idea. 'I dunno? An astronaut? Or maybe if I can't be that, a window cleaner?'

What do you want to be when you grow up is a lame question. It feels a little lazy. I prefer a tweaked version of the same question, which is a thousand times more powerful:

What kind of person do you want to be when you grow up?

I knew the answer to that at age nine, and 15, and 37 and 56, and I still will at age 95 and three quarters. For me, it's deadly simple: I want to be the best me I can be.

I'm guessing your answer will be similar. You want to be a nice, kind, loving, positive, optimistic, honest, good, grateful, friendly, happy, successful human being.

But there's one more word that is super-important. I'll get to it via a little story I wrote called 'Real or Fake'. Here's a snippet:

Jake was in wondering mode. He was trying to work out what he preferred, so he wrote a list called real or fake, and it went something like this …

Orange flavour, or an actual orange?

Freshly ground coffee or instant?

Mr Whippy or Ben & Jerry's?

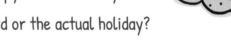

A postcard or the actual holiday?

Fake lashes or real?

Coca-Cola or supermarket brand cola?

Raw or photoshopped selfie?

Blackpool Tower or the Eiffel Tower?

A real flesh-and-blood friend or an online 'friend'?

A trip to see Santa in Lapland or at the local department store? (obviously, if you're under 10, they're both real)

Astroturf or lush Wembley grass?

Monopoly money or real cash?

A fake smile or a heartfelt grin?

There's more but I'm hoping the penny is beginning to drop.

Okay, it's not totally clear cut. Fake lashes and nails... they might be better than the original? And your selfie might actually look more attractive if you let the filter work its magic?

But generally speaking, the real thing is nearly always better than the cheaper or fake alternative.[4]

Think about it, I'll give you a real Van Gogh to hang on your bedroom wall, or a £10 print off the internet. Real or fake? The difference is priceless!

My point is that there are a lot of things that you can fake in life. In fact, you can almost fake life itself. Which brings me back to the original question: *What kind of person do you want to be when you grow up?*

I want to be real. I want to be authentically me.

It's easy to pretend to be somebody you're not. It's even easier to live as a pale imitation of yourself. It's easy to make excuses as to why your life hasn't turned out quite as you hoped.

It's easy to settle for 'fine'.

Which is fine if 'fine' is what you want. But if you want to raise the bar to world class, if you want to take life by storm, that means no more fakery. No more pale imitation. No more settling for 'that'll do'.

No more excuses!

---

[4] For the record, I'd argue very strongly that the raw selfie is way more gorgeous than the airbrushed nonsense.

Truth, Justice and the American Way
What are you throwing away?

Oh just some old ideas and beliefs that were taking up too much space

Have you seen the first Superman movie, starring Christopher Reeve? I'm old enough to remember it being released into cinemas in the previous millennium. There was a lot of hype. The poster said, 'You'll believe a man can fly.'

Take a look on YouTube and make up your own mind! The special effects back then were not so special.

But there is a really cool scene from the original movie. It's night time and Lois Lane is standing on her balcony, 45 stories up, looking out over the city lights. Metropolis is twinkling. Superman flies down and lands on her balcony. She looks stunned, and for good reason. After all, this is a guy in a Lycra suit, wearing his underwear on the outside. Oh, and he can fly!

Lois is a reporter and can't let go of her journalistic instincts, so she asks him, 'What do you stand for, Superman?'

Our hero puffs out his chest with pride before announcing, 'Truth, justice and the American way!'

As sickly and cheesy as that may be, I rather like it, because at least he knew! At least he could quote a set of values. We don't need to have the same beliefs and values as Superman and we certainly don't need to wear our underwear on the outside, but knowing what our values are is a fine starting point.

Typically, most people aren't that closely connected with their values, and because of that, they can easily get caught up in activities that are not truly meaningful to them.

Values are like a compass. They will guide you but sometimes you might get a little lost. Which is fine. Life has many paths. There are right ways, wrong ways and in-between ways. When you feel lost, go back and consult your values - they will bring you back on track.

To stop you getting lost, I'm suggesting you spend some time tuning into your values.

Activity: Values Grand Slam

The Values Grand Slam activity is challenging. It's designed to help point you in the right direction.

In the 'values challenge', you get to choose the winner in each round. There are some tough choices. Choose wisely.

When you reach your final 4, reflect on how they might guide your actions.

★ Values Challenge

Friendship

Competitive

Resilient

Belonging

Dedicated

Fun

Risk taking

Teamwork

Winning

Reliable

Loved

Loving

Gratitude

Learning

Excited

Calm

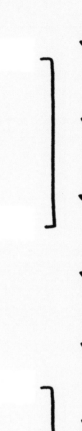

★ My Final 4:

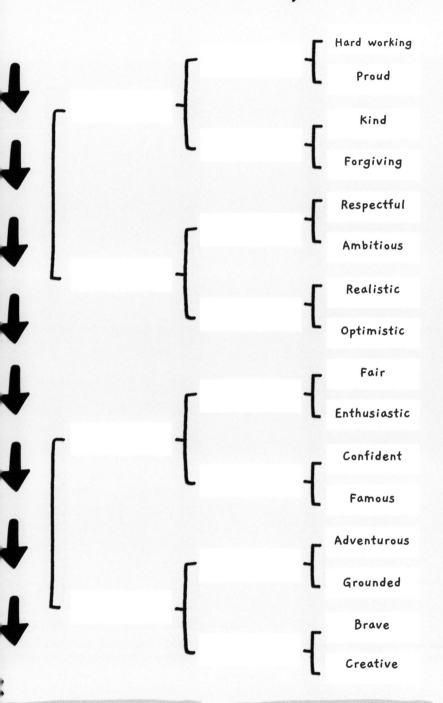

Hard working

Proud

Kind

Forgiving

Respectful

Ambitious

Realistic

Optimistic

Fair

Enthusiastic

Confident

Famous

Adventurous

Grounded

Brave

Creative

That's interesting,
because...

Explanation 12.
Growing Pains
Truth of the day:

Your teenage years are less like an ocean cruise and more like white water rafting.

Naked and screaming!

Just so you know, at the time of writing this book, the cost of raising a child to the age of 18 is £208,736. That's the basic, no-frills, heating, clothes and food price. If we add in luxuries such as toys, haircuts, holidays, tech and 15 years of education, it's eye-watering.

So, when your mum got pregnant, she was landing herself with a bill for a *minimum* of £208,736. While that sinks in, let's go back to your original birth day, the day you arrived into this world.

I'll spare you the graphic details in case you're reading this at breakfast time. Suffice to say, the day you were born, things got messy and your mum worked really hard, so it might be worth giving her a hug and saying thank you, right now!
You popped out, naked and screaming, covered in gunk. Someone rubbed a sponge over you. Then you were wrapped in a towel and handed to your mum. In everyone else's eyes, you were a bald baby alien with bits of slime in your ears, but to your mum, you were the most beautiful thing in the entire world.

To be fair, you still are.

It was love at first sight. You to her and her to you.

GIVE THE GIFT OF LIFE

Available for pre-order. Best-seller. HUMAN BABY

All **HUMAN BABY** varieties come pre-programmed with unconditional love and arrive in rapid learning mode. **HUMAN BABY** can be programmed to speak any language. Adaptable to most environments. **HUMAN BABY** can be trained to walk and talk within ONE year and toilet trained in two years (models vary).

Several skin tones to choose from. HUMAN BABY comes in traditional girl and boy models, or our brand new non-binary edition.

HUMAN BABY comes factory fitted with cuteness. Special features: chubby cheeks, gurgling and dribbling.

Order your HUMAN BABY today and get these extras:

Sleep mode

Awake mode

Cry mode

Cry for no reason mode

Wake at 3 a.m. mode

Nappy filling mode

Projectile-vomiting mode

Available in various sizes. Standard delivery is nine months, but small ones can arrive early.

Starter price: £208,736

No refunds. No warranty. No questions asked. No training required. Luxuries (haircuts, toys, education, etc.) not included.

(Please leave a note if you're not in and we can leave **HUMAN BABY** with a neighbour)

But if we pause and think about that moment of handover, your mum is being gifted the most precious thing in the world - a human life. Your parents' job is to nurture this tiny human being into a fully-fledged adult that will, one day, fly the nest and be capable of looking after itself in the wild.

Your mum gazed lovingly at her newborn, and you gazed lovingly back. This fledgling human being has a brain and emotions. It will develop a personality, with likes and dislikes. It will learn and unlearn. This tiny human will test its parents to the limits. The next 18 years of rearing will bring untold pleasure and pain, not to mention hundreds of sleepless nights.

But this gift of life moment isn't to be pondered and savoured. The health service is stretched to the breaking point. There's another woman contracting her uterus in the waiting room and she needs your mum's bed! So in actual fact, you are gifted to your parents and 90 minutes later, politely but very firmly, they're ushered out of the hospital door with a booklet of baby food vouchers.

Think about the magnitude of this moment. You are unique, a total one-off. You are the most complex piece of kit ever invented. You arrive into the world with a new pram and some discount food vouchers - but no instruction manual!

NO! instructions!!!

Your mum is literally making it up as she goes along. *Spoiler alert, she still is!*

Hence, can I ask a favour?

Whoever is bringing you up - mum, dad, step-mum, next-door neighbour, Aunty Brenda, werewolves - cut them some slack.

They are doing their best. I know it might not look that way, and sometimes they'll mess up, but now you've reached teenage-hood the complications just get worse. All the rules your parents learned during your childhood stage are now out of the window.

Teenagers work on a different operating system. You have needs and emotions. You have thoughts whizzing around your head and hormones pulsing through your system. Your body will be changing. Hair will be sprouting in unusual places. You have dreams, secrets, values, fears and feelings. Teenagers experience higher highs and lower lows.

You don't even understand you, so what chance do your parents have?

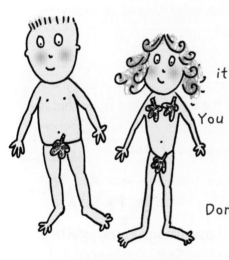

TOP TIP:
That body of yours,
it's given to you as a gift.
There's no receipt.
You can't return or exchange it,
so make the best of it.
Don't abuse it.
Don't exhaust it.
Don't leave it lying around in
the sun for too long.

The human operating system: zero to 12

There are 8 billion humans jostling for position on the Mario Kart leader board. We're all unique, but it turns out that there

original face

are some basic phases of development that we all go through. I'll be super-brief, but if you understand the headline news, it might help explain a few things.

When you were born you arrived with what Buddhists call 'the original face'. It's the pure version of you. No added flavourings or colourings. There was no pretence, no shame, no trying to impress. You were a blank slate, ready to be imprinted on.

The one-day-old version of you didn't know about gender, race or religion. You didn't know school existed. You didn't know about Mondays or Fridays, weekends, or rainy days. You didn't look at other babies and wish you had a cool car seat like theirs. You didn't worry that you had bulbous hamster cheeks or that you were bald.

Up until about eighteen months, babies have no sense of self. An infant can look in the mirror and not recognise itself. You were an experiencer. You squeezed the world, licked it, sniffed it, stuck your fingers in it... exploring, curious, questioning. As an infant your brain was a buzzing hive of connectivity.

You were also, by the way, full of love; when two-year olds meet other two-year olds, they hug, they share and they play.

From two to ten you became what psychologists call 'adult-centred'. Mum, dad, gran, they are like Gods. You hugged and worshipped them. Once you developed secure attachments with adults you had confidence to go explore your world.

Fast forward to right now. Up to this point you've learned how to walk, talk and control your bowels (fingers crossed on that one), but when the body strikes teenage o'clock the brain goes through a major re-wiring process.

How much you worry about what other people think of you

How often they do!

13+ Teens behaving badly
Teenage TLC

Your brain is shapeshifting. Your body is transforming. Teenagers need about 10 hours of good quality sleep, **every night.**

Sleep deprivation is the new saturated fat. Six Red Bulls is **NOT** the answer. Sleep is the answer.

Top tip to wake up feeling refreshed –**go to bed earlier!**

As you approach your teenage years your emotional system goes into overdrive. Cue a whole lot of classic teenage behaviours: social sensitivity, mood swings and self-doubt. These 'growing pains' might challenge you, but they don't have to defeat you.

Your brain squirts dopamine in big quantities. We seek out pleasure, we experiment and take silly risks. (I say 'we' because

LEGAL HIGHS...

 **clean laundry**

 **fitness**

 **fresh air**

foreign lands

Kindness

fulfilment

today

accomplishment

What are yours?

it's not just you. Anyone who's reached the ripe old age of 15 has been through the same).

The front part of the human brain is the last bit to develop. The so called neo-cortex (the bit above your eyebrows) plays two crucial roles. First, it enables you to keep your hat on and second, perhaps even more important, it enables rational thought. It's the thinking brain. Remember, this develops *after* your emotional system, which means your brain doesn't really have a handbrake in the teenage years. That's why teenagers stomp around not quite knowing what they're feeling, why they're feeling it, or what to do about it!

The teenage brain isn't very good at planning. That's why you forget your PE kit, can't find your bus pass, and leave your homework until the very last minute. Your under-developed pre-frontal cortex also means that you lack the higher order ability to act with consequences in mind. You follow the crowd (sometimes even when you know it's not a great idea), you question authority, kick back, push the boundaries and develop your own views and ideas about how the world works.

You're not right, but you absolutely think you are.

You become what psychologists call 'peer-group centred'. Teenagers experience an overwhelming desire to fit in. That explains why you dress the same as your friends. I'm guessing the same haircut too? Your tribe becomes all-important and your family can become very uncool. Your dad, who you worshipped last year, is now a bit of an embarrassment.

Developments between your ears are changing how you experience the world. Up until the age of about ten you didn't care what anyone thought about you. Think back to primary school, you'd stick your hand up to every single question and sing your loudest and proudest in school assembly. All of a sudden, you become a teenager and all that changes. You become self-conscious.

In simple English, you begin to imagine what others think about you.

And that's massive!

Let me say it again, slightly differently. Up until now it hadn't crossed your mind that anyone had an opinion of you. And all of a sudden, it dawns - you start having thoughts/opinions about other people and, BOOM, you realise other people are capable of having the same thoughts about you.

Yes folks, they're talking about you behind your back!

Self-doubt kicks in. That carefree version of you, the one that soaks up the world, the skipping, jumping in puddles, happy you, starts to hide.

Life becomes a 'fitting in' game. You become *hyper*-sensitive. You'll be blushing a lot. Don't take it personally, all primates go through these phases. There's not much you can do about them, but I thought it might be useful to know what's going on so next time you get embarrassed or you end up doing something stupid to fit in, you can blame evolution.

The good news is that most humans navigate the choppy teenage years perfectly well and things eventually settle down. Your brain is fully developed by your mid-20s and the vast majority emerge into the adult world just fine. As, I'm sure, you will.

Just to be sure, I've created an activity that will help you understand you a little bit better...

Getting to Know me

We've established that humans go through phases of development but we don't come with a detailed instruction manual. But imagine, just for a few minutes, that YOU actually did.

Imagine there was a page that summed up how to get the best out of YOU, and that this is THAT page. If you turned up at a police station with your memory wiped, this page would give the world some clues about how to get the very best out of you.

Now's your chance...

NAME:

....

Nickname:

....

Three words that describe me at my best:

☆

☆

☆

Things that A N N O Y me:

....

....

Things I love to do: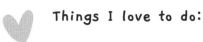

....

....

People I love to do these things with:

PROUDEST moment so far:

....

....

FAVOURITE TV programme:

....

....

Feed me this and I'll be your friend forever:

....

 DON'T feed me this:

....

Music that's guaranteed to make my foot tap and my bottom wiggle:

....

....

Don't make me listen to this:

BEST qualities:

TOP three personal strengths:

→

→

→

If I had to watch ONE movie over and over again, forever, it'd be this:

I tend to cope **better** when...

I tend to cope LESS well when...

If you want to get the best out of me, this is how I prefer to be treated:

HUGE AMBITION:

#BrilliantTeenager #GrowingPains #GrowingGains #KeepYourHatOn

Clause 13.

The ONE thing

Growing uUP

Be the kind of learner your teacher wants you to be. Which is...

And while you're in the mood, let's take it to the next level. You may as well be the kind of person YOU want to be. Which is...

The irony was lost on Mel. This was the first thing She'd ever won!

Numero Uno

I love doing school assemblies. Teenagers are great but primary schools are where the magic sauce is.

It's a wonderful sight as hundreds of children pour into the hall, and arrange themselves in date order, with the tiny ones at the front and the biggies at the back.

Bottoms on the cold floor, legs crossed, backs straight, waiting to start. One of the little ones is always picking their nose and showing it to their neighbour who always looks super-interested, nodding in approval.

And I try and picture chimpanzees doing the same. I'm no expert but I don't think our closest relatives in the animal world have assemblies? I mean, maybe they do? Every morning the chief chimp assembles the troop for a bit of a chat and a sing song and to give out some certificates, but I've never actually seen it in the wild.

So I have to imagine it. Three hundred chimps pouring into the hall on a wet Tuesday morning. Picture the scene. It'd be chaos. They'd be chasing each other around the hall, climbing the curtains, thumping some sort of random monkey tune on the piano and throwing poo at me.

I promise you, I've visited some tough schools, but none quite as bad as that! Because, by and large, humans have learned to behave and get along. We have rules and standards and ways of behaving.

So here's a question for you... what do you think is the most important quality you can bring to school? The ONE and only rule. The actual number ONE. The thing your teachers need you to be. The ONLY thing they really need...

Manners maybe? Positivity certainly helps. An open mind? Good behaviour - yes please.

Helpful, clever, friendly. I guess listening is important too, and maybe working in a group.

Having the courage to put your hand up and give things a go. Yep, teachers value that for sure.

All the things I've just listed are important. But I'm looking for something else. The x-factor. The ONE thing...

The actual number ONE thing your teachers need you to be...

Is....

TO BE TEACHABLE.

Yes, it's ever so simple. Be teachable. That's it!

If you bring that, everything else falls into place. All the other stuff I just threw into the mix - manners, listening, group work, open minded, positive, helpful, good behaviour - they are part and parcel of being teachable.

You might have heard of growth mindset. Making mistakes and learning from them - that's also part of being teachable.

In fact that's a BIG part of being teachable.

Here's something that nobody ever tells you about growth mindset and 'teachability'... it makes school so much more interesting. Once you become teachable, you become a good learner, you fall in love with learning and it's like rocket fuel for your future.

So make the effort to become a good learner.

Get into the habit of being a good learner. Day, after day, after day, after day, after day...

... after day.

Being teachable will literally change your life.

It can take you from bottom of the class to top really quickly. Or it can take you from middle of the pack to extraordinary. Or it can take you from top of the class to top of the world. It can take you to the best university or to your dream career.

The truth... it doesn't matter what anyone else is doing. It matters what YOU are doing. So do yourself a favour and demonstrate the habits of being teachable.

just do
this!

Which are:

Rock up on time.

Sit like you care.

Behave like you can.

Show up with the right attitude.

Work like you mean it.

Be bothered.

Have respect.

Listen with enthusiasm.

Being teachable is like flicking an attitude switch. It has an amazing side effect. When you fall in love with learning, your teachers fall in love with teaching. But best of all, when you're teachable, I'm excited for your future!

Notes...

Lightbulb Moment 14.
SUCCESS: The Cheat Code

Success

what people think
it looks like

Success

what it really
looks like

How to make your dreams come true

Most people imagine that being an author is a pretty cushy job. I mean, all you've got to do is write a few sentences and, hey presto, your day is finished and you can go laze by your swimming pool sipping mojitos, bossing your staff around and counting your money.

It's not quite as cool as described above, but there's no doubt it is an epic career.

So let's compare and contrast the chances of two children growing up and becoming a best-selling author.

Scenario 1. Imagine Kid A, age nine, with a burning ambition to be an author. That child reads and writes for fun. They're devouring big grown-up books while still in primary school. They step up to big school as a straight-A student, and go on to study English Literature at one of the top Universities. Basically, from age nine, Kid A has lived, breathed and pooped books.

Meanwhile, in Scenario 2, the merest inkling of a thought about writing books has never entered Kid B's mind. I mean, why would it? The kid doesn't even like reading or writing. That child drifted through school, achieved an eye-watering level of mediocrity, failed their English exam, and worked in a factory. Twenty years later Kid B has grown into Adult B and has not read a single book since leaving school.

I'd love to be able to tell you that I'm Kid A - that I had a big dream, worked super-hard, had grit, determination and eventually won through and nailed my lifetime ambition. Happy ending. Dreams really do come true. *Hooray!*

But I can't. Because I'm Kid B.

The chances of me ever becoming an author were laughable, which begs the question, how?

How the heck did I create a career out of nothing?

The answer, I got HUGGy. Hang in there, let me explain...

Supersize your goals

It's important to understand that 'success' isn't a straight line. Success looks rather like a plate of spaghetti bolognaise. You stick your fork in, whirl it around and slurp some in.

It's a bit hit and miss and, yes, success is messy!

In terms of achieving amazing things in your life, my advice is to set huge goals. I cannot think of a single breakthrough in humankind that would ever have been achieved with a tiny weeny goal. For example, space travel would never have been achieved by thinking 'realistic' and 'achievable'.

Huge achievements need huge goals, so I think goals should be

huge.... and small.

Confused? Let me explain.

You should super-size your goals. Here it is in a single sentence: If you want to achieve amazing things in your life, then you have to elevate to HUGGs - Huge Unbelievably Great Goals.

A HUGG is something that inspires and excites you. It's on the edges of your achievability. It's something that isn't going to happen by accident; it happens because you *make* it happen.

You have to step into best-self mode and ask yourself some searching questions:

First, what do you want to achieve in the next year, two, five, maybe ten years? Clue: it has to be something edgy, exciting and worth getting out of bed for.

Second, you visualize your huge goal in great detail. What does it look, sound and feel like? Smell it. Taste it. Snuggle into the feeling of having achieved it.

Third, what are the steps to getting to where you want to be?

And last, have you got the courage to take some action?

Here's the HUGG pyramid that was introduced to me by the goal-setting guru, David Hyner.[5] It literally changed my life.

[5] Check Dave out at https://www.davidhyner.com/

HUGGy instructions

You start at the top. The only rule is that what you write as your Huge Unbelievably Great Goal has to have the wow factor. It has to ignite the fire in your belly.

Once you're worked out what your HUGG is, it's game on. The thing about HUGE goals is exactly that. They're HUGE! In fact they might be so GINORMOUS that it's hard to know where to start, so the next step is to go to the bottom layer of your pyramid and start to fill in the small things that you have to do *every single day* that will move you forward.

I call the individual blocks SUGGs: Small Unbelievably Great Goals. The bottom layer is all about daily habits. It's about creating the version of you that shows up every day.

Then fill in the things you have to do to get 'half way' and 'nearly there'. Give it some serious thought. Fill in *all* the blanks. Colour them in!

With all the sections of the pyramid filled in, stick the thing on your bedroom wall and look at it every day. Something exciting will be staring right back at you, the massive goal and the steps to your ambition.

No excuses! *It'll be in your own handwriting!*

HUGGs and SUGGs. They'll take you one step beyond.

It's goal-setting MADNESS.

And I'm telling you about it because it works.

Pass it on.

Remember, people will judge you by your actions, not your intentions. You may have a heart of gold – but so does a hard-boiled egg.

Anonymous

Less conversation, more action!

But there's more. Ultimately, the difference between setting one of those normal boring objectives or a HUGG boils down to this: in terms of goals, are you interested or committed?

For example, you can be *interested* in becoming a vet, you can be *interested* in getting a place at a top university, you can be *interested* in developing your own app, you can be *interested* in becoming a professional footballer, you can be *interested* in getting stellar grades, you can be *interested* in getting in shape, you can be *interested* in working hard, you can be *interested* in being your best self...

My point? There are a lot of people *interested* in achieving amazing things. The talkers.

HUGGs are for the *seriously committed*. The doers.

Huge goals provide you with a powerful cocktail of willpower (which gets you off your backside) and way-power (which gives you something magnificent to aim for so you stay off your backside!).

Bottom line? For too many, the human race is a lifetime sprint towards mediocrity. Quit that particular race. Stop wasting your motivation on small stuff.

Get committed. Go LARGE.

Stop trying!

It's easy to play small. It's easy to NOT achieve your full potential. It's easy to talk yourself out of going for your dreams – it's too difficult, I'm not clever enough, it'll take too long, what if I fail?

Go back and re-read the School of UN-Learning chapter. Those pesky bananas. You need to let them go. Remember, to surge ahead you need to get into good habits and OUT OF BAD ONES. That means it's worth pondering what you're willing to give up to achieve your ambitions.

That's a much bigger question than it sounds.

As is this: What kind of person do you need to be to achieve your huge unbelievable great goal?

I'll leave those biggies hanging and sign off this chapter with a bunch of bananas you didn't know existed. I'm burying my advice right here, randomly, in chapter 14, to hide it from your parents and teachers because they'll absolutely hate this next bit. It goes against everything you've ever been taught.

In the interests of challenging you, my first banana dropping tip... come closer cos I've got to whisper it...

... you need to stop trying!

Please note, I'm choosing my words very carefully here. For the record, I'm all for effort. The 'EF-word' is not just an ingredient in success – it's the ingredient.

So please aim for an A for effort. But a Z in trying.

I hate the word 'try'. It ruins everything!

My life has blossomed ever since I stopped using the word 'try'. Unbeknown to me, that niggly little word had wheedled its way into my book of excuses. I had the best of intentions. I was most definitely a trier. I'd tell myself things like:

I'll *try* and get my book written, I'll *try* and get in shape, I'll *try* and eat healthier, I'll *try* to go to bed earlier, I'll *try* to be more confident...

And I'd fail every time because of that piddling three-letter word!

So I ditched it. I literally stopped trying. That was 20 years ago, and to this day, I still don't try, and my life is epic!

If you go back to the sentences above and delete the word try, they read thus:
I'll get my book written.
I'll get in shape.
I'll eat healthier.
I'll go to bed earlier.
I'll be more confident.

All of a sudden, the words have changed from wishy-washy, half-hearted, half-baked things I'd quite like to do, into steadfast promises I'm absolutely going to do.

I've gone from interested to committed.

#QuitTrying

→Word swap←

Maybe there are people who can achieve incredible success overnight. I don't know any of them, and I'm certainly not one of them.

But here's another small word change that will smooth the way. It's easy to slip into habits and routines and even easier to feel put-upon. You have chores or homework or things to do that you don't want to do. And, if you're not careful, these 'have tos' can start to weigh you down...

I *have to* get out of bed. I *have to* do my homework. I *have to* go visit my great gran. I *have to* go walk the dog. I *have to* set the table for tea...

Here's a **top tip** that works for me. I swap *'have to'* for *'get to'* and, all of a sudden, these activities become a joy.

I *get to* get out of bed - because I have a lovely snuggly bed, with a duvet and I'm not sleeping in a cardboard box.

I *get to* do my homework, because I'm getting an education.

I *get to* visit my great gran - because she's alive and well.

I *get to* walk the dog - because our family's got a pet.

I *get to* set the table for tea - because I have a family, and food.

So please stop *having to* do things. *Getting to* do them will make a bigger difference than you think!

Argument 15.
Ready. Aim. SPEND!

Activity:
The power of 'I AM...'

Your ego is your identity. It's who you think you are. All too often we talk down to ourselves; I'm not confident, I'm not as smart as my best mate, I'm not as good looking as so-and-so, I'm rubbish with numbers.

Once you assume that identity, you become that person!

To upgrade to a better version of you, you need to change your 'I AM' statements to something more inspiring.

I AM confident.

I AM smart.

I AM beautiful.

I AM capable of becoming good with numbers.

Basically, whatever follows 'I AM' will come looking for you.

This is too powerful to be left hanging, so I'm leaving space for you to write your own ten positive I AM statements.

1

2

3

4

5

6

7

8

9

10

REMEMBER, you become what you believe so whatever follows 'I AM' will seek you out. 'I AM' will chase you down. It will catch up with you and you will become 'I AM...'

So it makes sense to upgrade your I AMs.

Gratitude

Take a dose every Morning

May cause shifts in perspective

May cause feelings of abundance

Decreased feelings of fear and anxiety

An attack of the gratitudes

Life is a contact sport. Growing up can be especially trying what with exams, relationships, hormones, body changes and fitting in. Every young person in history has experienced these pressures.

It just so happens that the modern world has piled even more weight onto the shoulders of young people. Social media, airbrushed perfection, celebrity culture, the pressure to look good – it's easy to develop 'comparisonitis'. You look around with envy. Everyone else's life looks better than yours – they have a bigger house, more exciting holidays, more expensive trainers, a smarter phone, a nicer smile, better hair, more friends, better grades, a better school bag, a perfect family...

It can feel as though the Lamborghini of life has left you in its dust storm.

So here's a quick and obvious win.

Your brain is really good at noticing bad stuff. Humans are literally hard wired to spot things that are scary, dangerous and unexpected. As a result, it's easy to become fixated on all the things that are missing in your life, or all the things that could go wrong. To stop your brain over-heating with worry, it's worth training yourself to do the exact opposite, which is to notice the good.

One of my biggest leg ups to happiness was to adopt an attitude of gratitude. In an age of anxiety, you can begin to turn the tide away from a panic attack by having a 'gratitude attack'.

I learned how to wake up to the magnificence of being able to sit up in bed, rub the sleep from my eyes and engage with the miracle of existing on a planet with a breathable atmosphere, Coca Cola, wi-fi and great music.

Heart beating? *Check* ✓

No toothache? *Check* ✓

Sit-down toilet with flushing action? *Check* ✓

Hot shower? *Check* ✓

Fluffy towel? *Check* ✓

Wardrobe full of clothes? *Check* ✓

Decent breakfast? *Check* ✓

Hot drink from favourite mug? *Check* ✓

Loving family? *Check* ✓

Functioning eyeballs? *Check* ✓

Ability to read? *Check* ✓

Free education? *Check* ✓

You get my drift? Gratitude is like fertilizer for happiness. It's one of the quickest and simplest of happiness hacks.

As with most of my top tips there's something extra coming, but meantime, why not have a go at writing your gratitude list. In the space on the next page, write a list of 20 things that you appreciate but take for granted. Basically, what are you incredibly lucky to have, but might have taken your eye off?

I'm asking you to list at least 20, but you don't have to stop there (a 14-year-old girl once listed 187 things in 10 minutes).

My #GratitudeAttacKtop20

Keep this list by your bed. Look at it in the morning when you wake up. Holy mackerel, you're so lucky! Look at what you've already got!

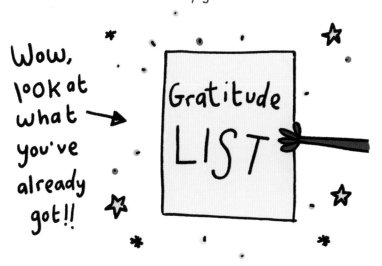

Developing an attitude of gratitude is a much bigger deal than it sounds. Once you've mastered it you'll be living in exactly the opposite way to most people. Most people spend their entire life grumbling about what they haven't got. Your mates will want designer clothes, a smarter phone, nicer hair, a better school bag, the latest trainers...

Your parents will be chasing a better job, bigger car, nicer house, a fancy holiday...

Most people spend their entire life chasing something bigger, better, faster, newer, flashier, sexier... we want more, more, more!

Check your gratitude list. Here's a thought - what if you've already got everything you actually need to be happy? What would happen if you focused on what you have got rather than moaning about what you haven't got?

Like I say, just a thought.

The seven great wonders of the world:

1. To see

2. To hear

3. To touch

4. To taste

5. To feel

6. To laugh

7. ...and to love.

Help! I'm Stuffocating!

Most people's happiness strategy is READY. AIM. *SPEND!*

Yes, I know that a new computer game, smartphone, laptop, pair of trainers, etc. will make you happy. But the happiness will quickly fade and you'll need to spend money again. If your happiness strategy is based on acquiring more stuff, it will always be short-lived.

Here's a sentence that, at first glance seems to make perfect sense...

... once I've got enough, then I'll be happy.

It seems true enough. Today's world makes us feel like we are not enough because we don't *have* enough. If you haven't got a smart phone, you want one. If you've got one, you want a smarter one. If yours is already super-smart you want a nicer phone case. So you buy whatever product it happens to be and, guess what, you do feel happy and shiny. Sometimes for a whole hour! And then there's another advert with another shiny happy person, and they've got a different product.

That must be what you need!

Some people chase 'more stuff' for their entire lives. Which makes perfect sense as long as you think that having more stuff makes you happy.

Every single ad on the TV, online or on a billboard is designed to make you unhappy with your life as it currently is. And we know this, right? We know that we're constantly being sold to.

We know what's happening, but we continue to let it happen!

Sold out!

you're the product

It's taken me a while to realize that with social media accounts, you and I are not the customer. The service is free. That means we're the *product*.

It takes a while for that nugget to settle. Basically, our attention is being sold. Your backstory, likes/dislikes/preferences, your friendship group, your clicks are being sold to marketeers. The social media 'customers' (i.e., the ones who pay the money) are the advertisers. Your data is mined. Algorithms are applied and a steady stream of suggestions comes your way.

Again, none of this is necessarily bad. It's how marketing has always worked. Just be aware. You are the product. More specifically, your *attention* is the product. Your attention has a price. If companies can snaffle your attention, you are more likely to buy their products and services.

Your attention is clickbait.

Are you stuffocating?

In terms of materialism, my message is to quit the chase. Less is more.

To be clear, I'm absolutely not suggesting that buying stuff is a bad thing. But there is something wrong with the crazy rate at which we've been consuming products. This planet of ours... Mother Earth... she's wheezing a bit. The forests are being cleared, orangutans re-homed and the oceans polluted so we can produce more stuff to buy/eat/wear.

It's important to understand that if there's something missing in your life, it's most probably YOU.

YOU at your best.

Once you discover that person, you can switch off your want-ometer.

Why? Because you at your best will learn to be satisfied with what you already have rather than lusting after what you haven't. Which brings me back to the sentence that started all this:

Once you have enough, you'll be content.

My wellbeing fact-checker reveals the exact opposite - when you're content, you'll have enough. What if true happiness isn't about chasing more, or wanting more? What if true contentment starts with being super-grateful for what you've already got?

I promise you this...

Once you're happy, you'll find you have more than enough stuff.

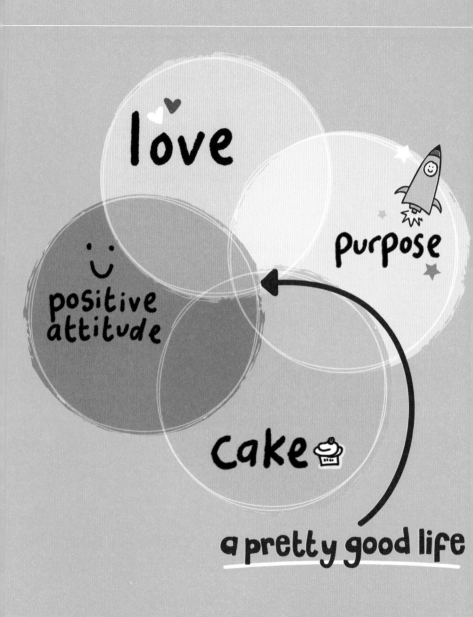

love

purpose

positive
attitude

cake

a pretty good life

Instalment 16.
Finding your WHY-factor

My 94-year-old nana is always reminding people that she is a great, great, great grandmother. I for one would have expected a little more modesty from a woman of her generation.
– Darren Conway, e-mail

Somewhere in a parallel universe...

The number 43 bus arrived and the lady showed her pass to the driver. He squinted at the picture, then the name, Joanne Katherine Rowling.

The doors swished shut, the bus pulled away and she stumbled towards a seat. The woman sat and watched the world go past. She was on her way to her perfectly nice office job. 'JK', as her colleagues called her, was a lovely team member. Not so good with numbers but pretty good with words.

JK's life was perfectly fine but she had a permanent knot in her stomach – she couldn't help feeling there was something missing. She sat in her usual seat and stared out of the window as the greyness of Edinburgh slipped by.

A few years ago she'd started writing a book. It was about a boarding school for wizards and witches. The main character was a boy called Harry Potter, but she'd created all sorts of wonderful friends and enemies and had given Harry what she thought was a terrific back story. His mum and dad had died and he lived under the stairs at his auntie's house, and then he got selected to go to this fantastic wizard school called Hogwarts.

She remembered back to when she was figuring out the plot. JK had been absorbed in her writing. She'd spent whole days in the coffee shop, tapping away at her laptop. She'd mapped the whole thing out. Harry Potter was an arc of a story that would be at least half a dozen books. In her wildest dreams she even dared to imagine a movie.

But that was then, and this was now.

She stood and pressed the red button, signalling the driver that this was her stop. The doors swished open and JK stepped out onto the pavement. She pulled her coat collar up and walked the final 50 metres to work. Her mind swirled with thoughts about Harry Potter. *Maybe I should have tried a bit harder?* she thought.

She remembered back to the time she'd shared her ideas with a friend. He'd just laughed. 'Seriously, JK?' he'd snorted, 'your hero lives in a cupboard under the stairs? And he's not good looking, or ripped?'

JK had been devastated, but perhaps he was right?

'And your spells have got such silly names. Everyone knows that magic is just plain old 'abracadabra'. Look JK, you're a good friend and I don't want to watch you waste your time dreaming about wizards and witches. I'm pretty sure that kids aren't going to want to read about a kid wizard battling with whatshisface – Moldy Wart?

'*It's Voldemort,*' she whispered to herself. But that was it. With her confidence gone, she'd shelved the whole Hogwarts project and had gotten on with her life.

The lift doors opened, she stepped in and the knot in her stomach tightened. It was a shame she'd shelved the Harry Potter series, but her friend's advice made sense. Dreams are for dreamers, right?

Thoughts about what you've just read

Dreams are for dreamers, right?[6]

---

[6] At time of writing this, J.K. Rowling's Harry Potter series has sold in excess of 500 million copies. Not to mention the films, theme park, studio tour and merch.

If you had an amazing gift to give the world, what might it be?

Describe the 'real' you.

Rage against the mundane

All of a sudden, at age 23, it struck Ravi. What became of all my potential?

Life is an opportunity - the question is, how to take advantage of it? Simon Sinek's Golden Circles diagram gives you a big nudge forward.

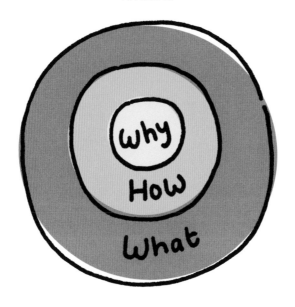

It can be applied to school, work or life. Let's have a go with 'school'. Most young people start at the outside of the diagram and work inward. And most people are fine with the 'what' and 'how' bits.

For example, if I asked, '*what* do you do?' you'd be able to answer me, most probably with something like:

'I go to school to do science, English, history and stuff.'

'And *how* do you do those lessons?'

'Erm, I sit and listen, mostly. Sometimes we do science experiments and we write stories in English.'

The crucial and often missing bit is the *why*. If I asked you '*why* are you learning those subjects?' you might struggle before offering something lame such as 'because I have to' or 'to get some good exam results'.

Simon Sinek suggests you work from the inside out. If you start with your WHY the 'how' and 'what' will look after themselves.

So, here goes.

'*Why* do you go to school?'

'Because getting a superb education is crucial to me making the most of my potential. School is an epic opportunity, handed to me on a plate, and I want to make the best of it.'

'*How* do you show up?'

'I do that by turning up to every lesson in "learning mode". Yes, even the boring lessons really matter because they show that I'm capable of sticking to tasks and getting on with people.'

'*What* do you do?'

'I rock up at school, being the best "me" that I can be.'

Shazam! You've found your 'why' and the fire in your belly will be burning hotter than the sun.

You'll hear a lot of adults grumbling about their job and how tough the world is. Listen to the moaners (there are plenty out there), but don't ever become one. The truth is they haven't found their purpose or their passion. They are in tune with the what and how, but their WHY is missing. It's as simple as that and has nothing to do with the economy, their boss, the government or anything else they may grumble about.

I'm going to share another grown-up point with you. You often feel tired, not because you've done too much, but because you've done too little of what sparks a light in you.

TOP TIP: Tune in to your WHY, find your passion, and then hang around with people who have found theirs.

Falling in love
with NOW is the
key to falling
in love with life
itself.

Question 17.

Who wants less on their mind?

It's all inside-out

Interesting question to ponder (and, in fact, the question that kick-started my research).

Could you be happier even if nothing in the world around you changed?

I'm not gonna lie, I nearly left this bit out but I figure that if you've come this far, you don't just want the golden egg, you want the goose that laid it.

Brain in gear. Strap yourself in. It's #GoldenGooseTime.

Depending on how old you are, I'm guessing if I asked you what stresses you out you'd say something like homework, assignments, family, boyfriends/girlfriends, the spot on my forehead, what to wear, the weather, what people think about me, the news, my wonky teeth, climate change, a spelling test...

And if I asked what makes you happy you'd say weekends, holidays, your family, your cat, ice cream, shopping, fresh air, nature, blue sky, picnics, cake...

These things are making us happy, or sad. Am I right, or am I right?

Actually, *I'm 100% wrong!*

What if I was to tell you that your emotions aren't coming from outside of you but, rather, every single feeling you've ever felt, and every single feeling you will ever feel, is coming from your thinking - in THIS moment.

You have to let that settle for a while because it changes everything. Inside-out thinking basically means that it's not your homework that's causing you to be angry. It's the way you're *thinking* about the 'unfair' amount of homework.

It's not the weekend that's making you happy. It's the way you're *thinking* about the ('woo-hoo, no school!') weekend.

It's not the person, thing, place or day of the week that's causing your feelings. *You're* causing your feelings. To be precise, the way you're thinking - *right now* - is causing you to feel the way you feel, *right now*.

Yes, I know it really seems like the world is making you feel angry, sad, jealous, confident, happy, miserable, joyful, grateful... it seems like that to me too. But it's actually the other way around. I'll say it again, because when you get it your life will change... *your emotions are coming from your thinking, in this moment.*

They always have and always will. I'm talking about 100% of your feelings, 100% of the time. I appreciate this might be challenging but there are no exceptions!

Unlocking a new level

I don't want to push too hard on this because you have to realise it for yourself, but let's step it up by applying inside-out thinking to the past and future.

We've all had bad things happen to us in the past. So, for example, lots of decades ago one of my teachers criticised me in front of the class. I was so hurt, angry and embarrassed that I can feel that bitterness welling up inside me right now.

So, hang on a second, how does that anger and embarrassment time travel from thirty years ago? How does that anger get into my body *right now?* Because I'm *thinking* about that comment *right now.* I think about it *now* - and I feel it *now* - even though it happened decades ago.

Future? Same! You can get stressed out about an exam that's coming up in 3 weeks' time. You feel anxious. You can't sleep. But again, how have those nervous feelings time travelled from 3 weeks in the future to inhabit your body right now? How can something affect you that hasn't even happened yet?

Answer: because you're *thinking* about your exam *right now.*

Your emotions are like a special effects department. They bring your thinking to life. Thoughts can be good, bad, sad, angry, jealous, grateful, ungrateful, loving, scary, positive, negative - but whatever they are, you'll be *feeling* them.

It's such a simple concept but the vast majority of people sail through life completely unaware of what I've just revealed. They fall for the illusion and just naturally assume that the outside world is doing things to them.

But inside-out thinking reveals the truth about Mondays, relationships, confidence, homework, exams, worry, guilt, shame, embarrassment... everything! The 'problem' isn't the problem. The problem is our misunderstanding about how emotions work.

It's not outside-in, it's inside-out.

This changes everything because it means the world isn't coming at you, it's coming *from* you.

BIG thoughts = BIG feelings[7]

TOP TIP:

If you keep getting electrocuted it's best to take your fingers out of the socket!

Inside-out thinking is humanity's best kept secret. Trust me, I know it absolutely 100% feels like Fridays are making you feel good, an Amazon delivery fills you with joy, an argument with your mum makes you annoyed, not being allowed to go to the party makes you feel angry, and that a film with a clown makes you terrified... but if we reveal what's behind the magician's curtain, you'll find it's all just thought weaving its emotional magic.

---

[7] This is a controversial section that goes against current thinking on therapy and counselling. Please read it carefully and with an open mind. Then read it again, more slowly. I am NOT suggesting that traditional therapy doesn't work, or is the wrong thing to do. If you are suffering from trauma and are in therapy, please continue to tap into professional help. This section is born of my frustration with the current psychological methods. I am merely daring to suggest there might be a better way.

Inside-out thinking is such a massive deal because the world is very full-on. You're learning to be an adult and it's a steep learning curve. Things are happening to you all the time, and some of them are BIG things. And because it's a BIG thing, you have some BIG thoughts about it. Most probably anxious, self-conscious, angry, negative, scary ones. If you're having those big thoughts a lot, guess what? You'll be feeling some BIG feelings.

Let me apply it to a simple situation. Imagine that last week you had to do a presentation in class, and speaking in front of everyone is your worst nightmare. You had no choice so you did it, but badly. You were shaky, mumbly and blushing. Presentation finished, you slunk back to your seat.

Today, when you reflect on last week's presentation, you feel embarrassed and shameful. It sure looks like the presentation is dragging you down. Anxious thoughts are swirling around your head while you sit through history and English. *How can I avoid doing presentations in the future? What will people be thinking about me? Why am I so rubbish?*

When you 'get' the true nature of inside-out thinking you realise that the episode happened last week. The presentation is finished. The only way you can feel embarrassed *right now* is because you're thinking about last week's trauma *right now.*

Apologies for the bluntness, but that presentation is finished. It's history. The only place it's alive is in your thinking, *in this moment.*

There are two big reveals. First, the trauma is kept alive by your thinking, and second, *you are the thinker.*

Note: I've used the word 'trauma' here because there are genuine traumas that happen to good people. Traditional therapy invites you to think about your trauma, discuss it, reflect on it... which makes no sense whatsoever because every time you think about it, you are re-living it, and those same terrible emotions are invited back into your body. Some people are in therapy their entire lifetime, re-telling and therefore *re-experiencing* their childhood traumas.

Inside-out thinking doesn't suggest the trauma never happened, it just reminds you that thinking about it over and over again means you're re-experiencing it over and over again. The terrible event happened, in the past. To repeat the exact same blunt truth from a few sentences ago, that trauma is finished. It's history. The only place it's alive is in your thinking, *in this moment.*

Here's the biggest question in a book of big questions. What if traditional therapy and counselling have gotten it backwards? The therapists' argument seems to be that you have to re-visit your trauma in order to process it. You're encouraged to chat about the pain, maybe re-think how you think about it until you can eventually put the episode behind you.

Common sense tells me the trauma is already behind you! It happened *in the past.* It doesn't make much sense to keep going back to it. I'm pretty sure your trauma was pretty bad at the time, so why on earth would you want to re-experience it a thousand times?

I'll come clean with you. Although I understand this, I still sometimes forget. But, generally speaking, my understanding of inside-out thinking (that my emotions are coming from my thinking *in this moment*) has allowed me to live a calmer life. When I do get grumpy about a late train, or upset by my father-in-law's dementia, or angry about how someone's treated me, inside-out thinking gives me options.

I can:

A. Choose to continue to think grumpy and/or upsetting thoughts. (Hey, this is the real world. Sometimes it's perfectly okay to have upset feelings).

B. Re-think my thinking and source a more helpful thought.

C. Notice that they're just thoughts. Choose to let the negative ones float past. Don't take them so seriously. Or personally.

D. Understand that this is how *all* human experience is created.

Option A is easy, which is why most people do it. Negative thoughts loop around their head and they stomp through life with grumpy boots.

B is useful, but re-thinking your thinking requires some effort.

C is mindfulness. It's *really* useful, but requires some practice to let the critical thoughts float on by.

Option D is a game-changer. You've cracked the code. Once you realise that your mind is just doing what minds do - *oh, that's how it works!* - you begin to relax into life. If every feeling is coming from your thinking, right now, it gives you a level of insight that most mortals simply don't have. When your mind jumps in with a bunch of insecure thoughts and feelings (which it will!) you recognise them as nothing to take too seriously. While most people will continue to have a lot on their mind, you'll have less. Once you've got a clearer head, with less mental clutter, it opens up space for solutions, ideas and fresher, nicer thoughts.

... and hey presto, positive feelings will flow from the *inside-out*.

> 'Yesterday's the past, tomorrow's the future, but today is a GIFT. That's why it's called the present.'

Master Oogway from *Kung Fu Panda* (although, to be fair, he borrowed it from others before him)

In case you're struggling with this point, let's work the same thing backwards. Think back to happy, joyous times and the chances are they were when you were not thinking about your weaknesses, or the drizzle, or homework, or the spot on your chin, or that Stacey has more social media followers than you do, or the unfairness of life...

That's why things like art, music or sport are great. If you can absorb yourself in a hobby, your thoughts will be focused on something positive and you will feel amazing.

Remember this: You are confident. You are grateful. You are loving and kind. You are all of these things, but with the power to think that you're not.

You feel amazing when your thoughts are amazing.

Amen.

I LOVE YOU

That will be all for today.

Thought 18.

Priorities

Here's a challenge. I want you to organise these 5 things into priority order. No cheating or over-thinking, just total honesty. There is no right or wrong and, chill, nobody's judging you.

In terms of 'importance to you' (and they're all important!), how would you rank these 5 things:

Relationships. Success. Money. Happiness. Health.

1

2

3

4

5

Love actually

I did the previous activity with a bunch of 14-year-olds in Birmingham and they debated, argued and engaged. Some went for money as their priority *('Because if I had money I could buy all the others, sir')* but most went for relationships, health or happiness.

I was about to move on when one of the lads raised his hand and said, *'Sir, you've missed something off the list.'*

I looked at the 5 words emblazoned on the screen and then back at the lad with a furrowed brow. *'What do you mean?'*

'Love, sir. If you add love to the list it changes everything.'

And 230 teenagers nodded in agreement. It's love, actually.

So, in case nobody's told you today, I love you, and I always will. Please hold that thought because it's the truth.

But I can't allow myself to write a book without telling you the whole truth, including stuff you might not like hearing.

There's something I've noticed. It's started fairly recently and it's difficult to say without it coming out wrong. But here goes anyway...

Young people are getting attached to a diagnosis. In some cases, people *want* a diagnosis. When a professional medical person tells you there's something wrong with you, you believe them.

Once you've been labelled with a disorder it becomes your identity and you act out that script in your head. It becomes who you are. For example, *I'm Andy and I need fixing!*

Take anxiety as an example. It's becoming a very common label. Anxiety comes in various flavours - general, social, obsessive compulsive, phobias, post-traumatic, panic, body dysmorphia - each with escalating levels of seriousness.

You might need to sit down for this bit.

I doubt there's very much actually wrong with you. You haven't 'got' anxiety. It all stems from a misunderstanding about the human operating system. Please go back and re-read the previous chapter! Once you understand that every emotion you ever feel is coming from your thinking *in this moment*, you'll realise what anxiety truly is.

It's nothing to do with what happened in the past or what might happen in the future. Anxiety is about what's running through your head *right now*, in this moment. Quite often, the only thing that's faulty is that you don't understand the fundamentals of how the human experience is brought to life.

Every time you're feeling anxious it's because you're having a worrying thought, *in this moment.*

When you're feeling happy it's because you're experiencing a happy thought, *in this moment.*

Sadness, same. Shame, same. Jealousy, same. Joy, same. Pride, same.

Every single emotion you've ever experienced, *SAME!*

I absolutely get that people seek a diagnosis because that's the start of the repairing process, but how about playing around with my diagnosis. How about switching your thinking. Instead of what's wrong with you, try the exact opposite question: what's *right* with you?

Adopt that as your diagnosis. Become THAT person. Act out THAT script.

What makes you come alive?

Top tip: do more of that.

Admittedly, not everyone 'suffers' from anxiety, but there are plenty who do, so I'm including something that felt very weird to write.

I've penned a letter to Anxiety. I've written it on your behalf. It's basically a letter from you to Anxiety. Read it, and if you agree with the words, please sign it. If every young person on the planet signs up to it, we might start an anti-anxiety movement.

If you don't like it, or disagree with my words, that's fine. We've left a blank page in case you want to have a go at writing your own personal letter to Anxiety. The only rule is that your letter has to come from a clear and calm state of mind. It's a chance to give your side of the story and get the ground rules between you and Anxiety sorted.

If you want to write your own, I'd love to see it.[8] Meantime, here's my attempt:

Ahem [clears throat]

Dear ANXIETY,

It's Dr Andy here. This is a difficult letter to write so please excuse my clumsy words. I'm writing on behalf of

[INSERT YOUR NAME HERE

....]

because they weren't sure where to start. Neither was I to be fair, but here goes.

Anxiety, me and you practically grew up together!

At first I was grateful for you. You reminded me not to do stupid things. If it wasn't for you I'd probably juggle with chainsaws and have a pet tiger.

---

[8] Please email me your 'Dear Anxiety' letter to andy@ artofbrilliance.co.uk

So thanks, but no thanks. Now I realise you're just holding me back!

The worst thing about you, Anxiety, is that you have a nasty habit of keeping me awake at night! You make me imagine all the things that can go wrong and I end up dreading the next day.

But you create day-mares too. I feel worried or scared. You make my heart flutter (but not in a good way!) and I can feel dry mouthed and panicky. You have such a hold on me that sometimes when you come knocking I feel physically sick.

You stand around me like one of those burly bodyguards. I get that you're trying to protect me from danger, but really? Is chatting to a new human being really so dangerous? Is putting my hand up and risking getting the answer wrong really such a big deal? Is taking an exam really worth getting all worked up about? Is it really worth losing sleep over what someone posted on social?

You're not protecting me, you're smothering me. You're a drama queen — too quick to jump in, too quick to see things that aren't there, and too quick to think I can't deal with it when in actual fact, I can.

I'm on to you, Anxiety. I've realised that 99% of what I worry about never actually happens. All that panic! All those dry mouths and hot flushes! You put me on edge for no reason.

You're like a fart in a spacesuit. *I can't breathe*, so I'm evicting you.

I've decided to go from fast and furious to calm and curious.

All this time you've been trying to convince me that you come from the outside world, but my penny-dropping moment is when I realised you're in my head. You're just a *thought*. That means you're not even real! I'm the one who thought you up!

OMG, that's an immense realisation because if I'm the one who created you, I'm the only one who can uncreate you.

That starts by realising that I'm stuck in NOW o'clock. Everyone is! We can't escape from the present moment. So rather than worrying about the past, or fretting about the future, I'm committed to accepting each moment. If my entire life is lived in the present moment it makes sense to savour it and notice something good. If I'm snuggled into the present moment, I've connected with life, and you, Anxiety, are toast.

Rather than letting you make me think I'm not smart enough, good enough, confident enough or gorgeous enough, I've realised the truth. I'm all of those things.

And more!

Thank you for trying to take care of me but I'm better off without you. So slowly, one breath at a time, I'm letting you go.

They say that breaking up is hard to do, but I'm not so sure. I'm announcing to the world that we're officially NOT in a controlling relationship anymore and, know what? I feel better already!

Thank you for reading this letter, Anxiety. Sure, life will sometimes scare me, but it's not going to ruin me.

Freedom, here I come!

Yours rebelliously,

[INSERT YOUR NAME HERE

....]

[DATE ....]

"you only live once, but if you do it Right once is enough

Mae West
(American actress and Sex Symbol)

Ultimatum 19.

Emigrating to heaven

Which disease would you rather have...

A. Gray Brittle Death (appears as a disease in the short story 'The Color Out of Space') is where victims describe 'being drained of something' or 'having their life sucked out'.

B. Hawaiian Cat Flu (from Jim Davis's Garfield books), a rare disease whose symptoms include a craving for Hawaiian pizza, a compulsion to wear loud shirts and an inability to resist hula dancing.

Your mission, should you choose to accept it

Picture the scene...

The spaceship legs extend as it slowly descends into Trafalgar Square. There's a minute of earthly silence before the door hisses open, smoke billows out, and a ramp extends from the mist.

The pictures are beamed live across the world's news networks. Eleven billion people hold their breath as half a dozen little green creatures emerge from the mist and shuffle down the ramp (I'm guessing webbed feet and eyes on stalks, but I could be wrong?) where the Prime Minister meets and greets, before inviting them back to Number 10 for a brew, some sandwiches and a slice of sponge cake.

Welcome to Earth! No missiles, no guns, no nuclear nonsense. That's the beginning of Inter-Galactic peace, love and niceness, right there.

That's my mission.

And, as of now, it's reached as far as you.

FOOL neighbours into thinking that you've just returned from Mars by sprinkling paprika on your trainers.

– Rob Cottam, e-mail

Cloud 9

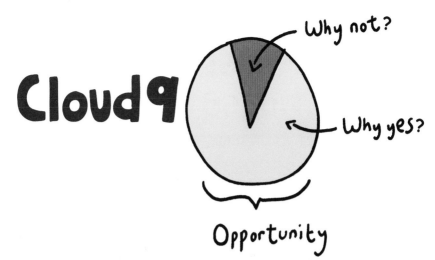

If we're starting an inter-galactic wellbeing ripple, I need recruits, and there's no time to lose.

The average earthling lives for about 4,000 weeks. You're a young person, so that seems like a decent amount of time, but go announce it to your gran and I guarantee she won't be laughing.

But remember, 4,000 weeks is the *average* lifespan. Some people get more, some fewer.

My finale contains the bluntest of truths - nobody gets out alive.

Literally. Nobody. Ever!

This book hasn't been about what you want to be. The subliminal question throughout has been, 'what kind of person do you want to be?' There are too many people having what I call an NLE, a Near Life Experience. I see them every day. If you were writing a school report on their life it would be a C+

They're living a *coulda, shoulda, woulda* life of *if only...*

And then, all too soon, just when they think they might have figured out the rules of life, their time is up. Nobody truly knows where you go when you die but for the sake of this final page please humour me and assume that we emigrate to heaven.

If you're not risking anything, you're risking everything!

In which case it's worth thinking about those who are already there. You might have loved ones who've passed away. Imagine them, sitting on their clouds, looking down on us as we go about our daily business. Remember, these are the people who've had their time. They've lived their lives. They know all about *coulda, shoulda, woulda.* They've experienced their own personal *if onlys...*

And they love you, which means they're rooting for you.

Let's get silly and play around with what they're absolutely not saying. They're unlikely to be advising you to play small. Your heavenly cheerleaders aren't yelling for you to take no risks or shy away from opportunities or challenges. They're not urging you to spend more time scrolling on your phone or playing on your console. They're not recommending that you put minimum effort into your school work or that you carry a mediocre attitude around with you. They're not bellowing, 'Frown baby, frown.' They don't want you to stay in bed until midday, and those up there are not recommending that you slouch around and only come alive at weekends. They're not demanding that you should be full of self-doubt and that you should eat junk food and guzzle sugary fizz.

The heavenly refugees have had their chance and they want you to make the most of yours! They're up there, screaming at you to go for it! Seize every single day! Take some calculated risks and go for opportunities when they show up. Get off your phone and look up, the world's amazing. Make eye contact with life. Smile. Be confident. Create friendships. Quit coasting. Lose the excuses. Work hard in lessons because those grades will open doors. Craft an attitude that makes people go wow. Get out of bed an hour earlier than everyone else and work on your secret long-term ambition. Eat the right foods, drink gallons of H_2O, get good quality sleep, because if you take care of your physical health you'll maybe eke out more than 4,000 weeks. It's okay to mess up. It doesn't matter if you sometimes fail or look silly. In fact, failure makes you stronger, and looking a bit silly is kind of sexy.

I 100% guarantee your heavenly champions are yelling for you to believe in yourself and squeeze the maximum value out of every single moment of every single day.

They're wanting you to make the most of your time down there because, hey, one day it'll be your turn to emigrate to heaven.

Until that day comes, commit to no more *if onlys*. Banish the *coulda, shoulda, woulda* mindset.

Back where we started!

The finale

Imagine you're 109 years old and, may I say, in very fine fettle. Must be that lifelong positive attitude and all that oily fish.

Imagine you're looking back on your life as it is TODAY, then finish the following sentences:

I spent too much time worrying about ...

I spent too little time doing things such as ...

If I could go back in time, then what I would do differently from today onward is ...

Congrats on your eyeballs reaching this far. And thanks.

I'm hoping you will have spotted the consistent message. If not, here it is in plain simple English. I'm suggesting that you quit comparing yourself with everyone else. Stop trying to match up to the prettiest, cleverest, sportiest, richest, most confident humans you know. While you're at it you may as well quit comparing yourself to the celebs and 'influencers' you don't know.

BRILLIANT TEENAGER has been encouraging you to be more of who you already are, at your best!

You v You is the only game in town.

Many pages ago we started with some truths, so it makes sense to come full circle. Here are my final four facts of life that just happen to have been the DNA of the entire book:

1. Upgrading to 'best self' means you're more likely to live your best life.

2. But it's bigger than that. If you live by example, I promise others will follow.

3. If you're going to create a ripple in the universe, there's no time to lose.

4. Start now, because now is all you have.

Ashleigh Brilliant: American author

Team biogs

Thanks for reading The Art of Being a BRILLIANT Teenager. If you've enjoyed it, please tell the world and copy us in. If you've hated it, please keep quiet!

Amy and I figure that being your best self is actually quite easy but *staying* there is tricky. We don't want to leave you in limbo so we've provided some wrap-around vids and activities that will keep you moving in the right direction.

Here's the QR code. You were born with a smartphone in your hand, so we're pretty sure you've got it from here.

Whatever life throws at you, we wish you an exciting journey.

Amy & Andy

Who the heck are Amy and Andy?

Here's a brief introduction to your very proud writing team

Back story. You know when you meet someone for the first time and something clicks?

It just so happens that Amy's dyslexic. She literally cannot spell 'dyslexia'. But, as is often the case, when you're not very good at something, your brain compensates by making you world class at another thing. What Amy lacks in words she makes up for in pics!

Andy's the opposite. He's art dyslexic. He can't draw for toffee. Or cakes or chocolate, or anything. But what he lacks in pictures, he makes up for in words.

When Andy's words met Amy's art, it was love at first sight. They share a common belief in fun and simplicity and have worked together on all sorts of books and creative projects.

Amy works from an art studio in Uttoxeter. She leads a double life as the creative director for a hugely successful training company in Derby.

Talk about spooky coincidences! Andy runs a hugely successful training company in Derby. He pivoted from being a successful children's author (his Spy Dog series was a massive global hit) into the science of happiness and wellbeing. Being able to look after your own health and wellbeing is the most important lesson you'll ever learn which is why his training company specialises in helping people step up to being their best selves.

Let's face it, what's going to be most useful to you in the next 80 years of your life, an understanding of

History or happiness?
Maths or mental health?
Geography or grit?
Art or attitude?
Computing or character?
Science or strengths?

Andy now works with the world's best creative director to bring happiness, wellbeing and resilience to businesses and schools across the world. I mean, how cool is THAT?

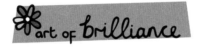

art of brilliance

WWW.ARTOFBRILLIANCE.CO.UK

EMAIL AMY: amy@artofbrilliance.co.uk
EMAIL ANDY: andy@artofbrilliance.co.uk